T0165168

Perceptions and Expectations

Career Advice on Surviving in the Working World

Eric Hinrichs

Archway Publishing books may be ordered
through booksellers or by contacting:

Archway Publishing
1663 Liberty Drive
Bloomington, IN 47403
www.archwaypublishing.com
1 (888) 242-5904

ISBN: 978-1-4808-7808-2 (sc)
ISBN: 978-1-4808-7807-5 (e)

Library of Congress Control Number: 2019907074

Print information available on the last page.

Archway Publishing rev. date: 07/05/2019

*To my wife, Kim, for believing in me
and to our greatest achievements,
Kara and Kasey*

Contents

Your Coworkers

Your Company

Preface

I HAVE BEEN in the workforce since 1971 when, at age thirteen, I had my first job picking up trash for one dollar an hour. Since then, I have worked in an auto store, a bookstore, a coal mine—between college semesters—as a process engineer, as a production supervisor, a draftsman, a tool and diemaker, a painter (dreadful job, and I was not good at it), a project leader, a quality engineer, a plant engineer, landscaper, blacktop layer, machinist, manager, auction runner, research and development engineer, and technical writer—not necessarily in that order.

Each job, whether it was a summer job or a job I held for years or months, taught me something and added to my experience and knowledge of the dynamics we call "work" and how we interact with coworkers.

A lot of my experience was earned the hard way through mistakes, personality clashes, ignorance, and economic woes—the usual suspects. However, my experience was not one-sided. I made mistakes like anyone else, but I also learned from doing the right thing and reaping the benefit of being considerate and sensitive to others' needs.

You might have experienced the same situations I have, or you may not agree with what I have written here; you may laugh at my thoughts, or you may find they don't apply to your career or company environment. Regardless, I wrote this book with the intention to help others, even if it's only one person, avoid the pitfalls I encountered and provide some insight that may help them accelerate their careers.

I feel that I learned some valuable, timeless lessons based on universal human nature and, thus, ones that will be relevant to some degree for some time. If I can help just one of you, I will be grateful that what I learned has been passed on and had a positive impact in someone's life so that recording what I have learned over the years will have been worth the time and effort.

I hope I can help you avoid suffering under a bad manager, avoid shooting yourself in the foot, and show empathy to those who are trying just as hard as you to become successful. We all take different paths through life, and experience comes in different packages. Having tolerance for differences *does* make a difference. The game of life can be tough. I suspect any help, any advice any of us can get, would be appreciated.

The chapters have been written to be read separately. Feel free to read straight through or as a chapter captures your interest.

Thanks for the opportunity to share.

You

1

Perception

WHAT IS PERCEPTION? It's one of those few words that suggest emotion. Perception is a feeling, an assessment, a gut reaction, emotionally or intellectually, to or about something or someone. It could be based on a myriad of factors. Sometimes we perceive intuitively, or our perceptions can be factual and absolute. Our impressions of an object or our reactions may be based on past interactions, judgments, prejudices, collective experiences, the environment, or social mores. Throughout our lives, we consciously or subconsciously judge others, objects, or situations. You will be judged against others and by others, as well as judging yourself. How tall or short you are, your appearance, your intelligence, what school you graduated from, regardless of how nice, mean, compassionate, rich, poor, or popular you are. You get the picture. Perception is judgment.

We can change our attitudes; sometimes that can be hard, but it's something we can directly control. And the perception of who we are in the eyes of others is largely based on our attitudes, the ways we interact with those around us, the ways we approach our jobs, and how we feel about ourselves.

Perception is why you size up people as soon as you meet them. Turning aside to your friend, you quietly say, "I don't think I like [insert name here]." It's true what they say about interviewing or when dating—you *do* form an immediate impression of a person. That's why you need to pay attention to details, to those incidentals you can control. Be in the moment and aware of what you are doing, how you are doing it, and where you are. This is also why you need to be careful of how you write emails, speak to those below, at, or above your level, write reports or give presentations, because these are also forms of expression and reflect on who you are.

For example, which email looks more professional to you?

Email A:
FRED,

THEIR IS NO WAY YOU CAN JUSTIFY THE VALIDATION OF PART 4653-14. THE DIMENSOINS DO NOT STACK UP, THE PULL FORCE IS WAY OFF. IT IS REDICULOUS TO THINK WE CAN ACCEPT THIS VALIDATION AS IT WAS CONDUCTED. I AM SETTING UP A MEETING TO ADDRESS THIS WITH MANAGEMENT. WE CANNOT MOVE FORWARD UNTIL THIS IS FIXED.
Kevin

Email B:

Fred,

I just reviewed the data you sent me from the validation of part 4653-14. It is great we finally completed the validation, but in reviewing the data, I believe we have a stack-up issue. When I looked at the pull-off force, they were not to specification. Can we meet to discuss? We may have to bring this to management's attention, but I would like to review the data with you and get your thoughts.

Thanks,

Kevin

See the difference between the two emails? They say the same thing, but the tone, the aggressiveness of the emails, is markedly different. One has spelling errors and is shouting at you in all caps. Which email do you think Fred would prefer to receive? Which email do you think reflects positively on you? Which email do you think establishes a positive rapport and relationship with Fred? Correct—email B. See how your perception was changed by how the email was written?

Everything we do in our lives has a basis in perception. We cannot fully control the perspective others have. Their perspectives are often a product of upbringing, life experiences, and their level of insecurity or self-esteem, or possibly, there is even a hidden agenda. We can evince the best possible appearance and attitude, which will at least give us a good chance of being accepted or perceived in the best possible light. Doing our best minimizes adding obstacles to overcome.

Gossip and Rumors

At work, pay attention to how you interact with your co-workers. How you dress, the cleanliness and neatness of your clothes, your hair, makeup, facial hair, the content, tone, and structure of your emails, your reports, how you comport yourself in meetings—they all have influence on how you are perceived. As a new employee, you're being evaluated every time you meet people or they see you. They're trying to figure you out. What are your strengths, who do you know, what do you know, what is your career direction, are you a rival, do they need to compete against you for that new position? Ever hear one woman say to another, "Hey, I love your outfit/necklace/scarf"? You don't think this is an indication that how you look is noticed? That your appearance reflects on a person's perception of you? It does, and people *do* judge. Everyone does, although to different degrees.

If you're a new employee, no one knows much about you. They don't know if you're "naughty or nice" (sorry, I am writing this part around Christmastime), or whether you are competent, who you click with, or how you speak. People are learning who you are, and the only way they can do that is by observing what you do and how you do it and what they hear through the rumor mill. So what do you want them to know about you? Understand about you? Like about you?

Perception is the key to advancement and a critical player in your ability to advance. You set the tone here and establish your own reputation, not anyone else. So take the time to really understand what you want and what you need to get there. People can only form their likes and dislikes by what you do and say—very much like the old saying "What you say is carried on the wind, and the wind touches all." Human nature being what it is, whatever you say eventually gets back to the person you were talking about. I find it easier not to comment on what others do or say but keep my comments to the work at hand. This way, my comments cannot be misconstrued. It's difficult to do this, but you do need to be aware that people use information to their advantage, not yours. If you're viewed as a rival, then most of what you do will be taken or presented in a negative light. There are a lot of individuals out there who thrive on gossip. Is this really an important point? It depends on what kind of people you work with.

Can perception matter? I had to deal with a negative perception of myself in a situation a long time ago. I worked where there was one guy who just loved to get the dirt on someone and pass it around. If I wanted something to get around, I knew all I had to do was mention it to him. I remember commenting in an offhand manner on something, and sure enough, the person whom I mentioned in the comment heard about it soon after. There was an awkward moment as I apologized and explained what I meant. This is an important lesson and not an easy one.

The same guy said something derogatory like, "I cannot believe so-and-so ruined the material. Any other person would have been fired for that, don't you agree?" This was a trap question. Why? Because he was trying to get me to agree to his statement, despite the fact that it was only speculation and just a casual conversation. He wanted a response from me.

Without thinking, I replied, "Yeah, he should have been." Sure enough, the guy spread the rumor that I'd said so-and-so should have been fired. He did not get into trouble, but I did. He just wanted to see what would happen to me for saying that, to create some controversy, create some friction. If I had just kept my mouth shut or maybe said something like, "I don't know.

It's not for me to say," then he wouldn't have had anything to work with, and I wouldn't have had to explain myself to the person or my manager, who called me into his office soon after.

"Eric," my manager said, "why are you saying so-and-so should be fired? I don't need you or anyone else going around making statements like that around here. You should know better than to say something like that." My manager would go on and on like that. It didn't matter when I explained that it was a side conversation, that I didn't know it would be repeated. You see, I'd said it, and it didn't matter why or where or when I said it … I said it. Who got into trouble? Not the guy I said it to in idle conversation, but me. Bear this in mind as you get to know people and try to recognize someone who gossips so you can be very careful what you say or do around them. Better yet, do not make comments about coworkers—it's much safer that way because gossip is never healthy, no matter your intentions.

I suggest you try to exercise restraint and refrain from commenting on others you work with. Your comments can easily be misapplied, be twisted to someone else's benefit, or get back to that person, and then you have more to deal with than just your projects. Sure, comment on what is going on regarding the tasks at hand, but stay away from commenting about your coworkers. Everyone has a right to speak about how something is being done, but making judgments about another person doesn't provide any benefit to you or your career—especially since some people have strong long-term memories. If they end up one day becoming your manager … well, good luck with that.

How you comport yourself is important; it's a lesson I found myself having to revisit even late in my career. Here's something else that happened to me that should help you see why your conduct is important to your career.

Emotions

I had been working at a company for many decades. I knew our products and the processes to make them very well. My expertise in these areas was helpful to teams in mapping out validations and changes. I was helping a project where a specification lacked a critical dimension. I advocated that this dimension was necessary to be defined since we were working to validate a second manufacturing site to produce the component and the workers at this second site needed to know what the dimension was to ensure product consistency. The current site didn't use the dimension, as the component was manufactured there for many, many years, so they just "knew" what the value should be. Unfortunately, the project was given to a project leader who had no knowledge of the component or process. Furthermore, he had no project leader experience. I identified the need for this dimension two years previously, but the manufacturing site didn't work on it since they "did not need it." The project leader felt it was not in the scope of his project and not his issue to deal with. He was in a time crunch and viewed this request as a roadblock to his timing.

Meeting after meeting dealt with the subject with no resolution and the project leader's culpable deniability. I was frustrated and annoyed by the ineptitude of the project leader. In a meeting held by telephone, the subject came up again with the same results, and I lost it. I basically chewed out the project leader in the call, told him it was his responsibility and he needed to own it, and as project leader, he needed to assign the resources to ensure the work got done within his time frame. He denied responsibility for all the above. That's when I said that these meetings were a waste of my time, and if he wasn't going to take ownership, I had other things to work on, and I hung up the phone.

Well, of course, I heard about this from my manager, other managers, directors, you name it. I committed a company no-no. How could I have yelled at the project leader? And I had also hung up on him! You see, it did not matter to management if the project leader was right or wrong; it was my disrespectful behavior that was in question. This was toward when the end-of-year and performance ratings were due, so management wanted to teach me a lesson and strip me down a level in performance rating. You see what happened here? I may have been correct, but my message was lost in how I handled the situation. Did I know better? Of course, but my frustration from months and months of dealing with this project leader and his denials of responsibility drove me over the top.

I somehow survived this issue, mainly due to my years with the company and my reputation (up until then!). What should I have done? I should have worked behind the scenes with managers and whomever else to educate them on the situation and have them push the right buttons to get the issue resolved. It wasn't one of my better moments, and I kick myself for letting my emotions get to me. What you need to know is there are other ways to respond rather than react and other avenues to accomplish what you wish done. You need to work the system rather than attack people and call them out on their shortcomings. If it were still early in your career and you did what I did, you might be looking for another job. Take this lesson to heart. Work the system, be calm, be specific, and communicate to your manager your concerns and needs. Keep your emotions to yourself. Getting angry does not serve you. Let others help guide you in finding a solution.

2

Expectations

When you think of expectations, do any of these come to mind?

- what your manager expects from you
- what your company expects from you
- what you expect from yourself
- what your family expects from you
- what your partner expects from you
- what your children expect from you

Our lives are full of expectations—those of our families, friends, coworkers, society, and ourselves. Expectation is what others believe they can count on you for or count on you to deliver. Too often, it's what they expect, not what you expect.

Your Team: You and Your Manager

Let's look at expectations from the perspective of work. Your manager expects you to complete a task by a deadline that was given to you. This is your manager's expectation of you. You expect to meet your manager's deadline because you agreed to it and you have personal pride (at least I hope so) in honoring your commitments.

The deadline comes and goes, and you fail to deliver as promised. Your manager expected you to have the work done. After all, your manager often asks you how things were going, and you always replied that everything was going well. Now your manager is not a happy camper. What's up? He or she wants to know. Why didn't you get it done? You gave your manager the impression that everything was going fine, and then you threw him or her for a loop; the manager doesn't know what to think now.

You reply with a lame excuse, falling into victim thinking. You knew you weren't going to get it done on time, didn't you? Why didn't you tell your manager the truth when you were asked how things were going? Of course, you said okay, because (a) you didn't want your manager to know and think you were incompetent, (b) you thought you could fix the problem in time and still make the deadline, and (c) you didn't think it was a big deal to miss the deadline.

How do you think your manager views you now? Do you feel he or she thinks highly of you? You just let your manager down, and now he or she will need to explain to their own manager what happened—and that, my friend, is not a good thing. You may have just messed with your manager's reputation with their own manager because they may have been communicating that everything was going well. But what about you? You think this helped you in your performance review? Think things will be smooth sailing for you? Of course not. The worst thing about this is you could have avoided the problem so easily, so very easily. Let's look at how this could have turned out differently.

What you could have done was to manage expectations. As soon as you became aware that you might miss the deadline or the potential to miss it was there, you should have started informing your manager. Do not wait until a scheduled meeting but ask for a minute of your manager's time to inform him or her. You don't want to wait to let your manager know of critical delays. This way, your manager is aware, will not be blindsided, and can start to manage expectations upward. Your manager is now in a position to help you with what may be causing you to be late. You could inform your manager along the lines of something like this:

> I'm trying to make the deadline, but I just ran into trouble with data downloads from manufacturing. I worked it out with manufacturing, and I'm expecting the data today. I can finish the analysis by tomorrow, but that means it's looking like Wednesday at the latest for the report. That is the best I can do given the delay in the data.

You see, you're creating a partnership between your manager and yourself. This is far better than the earlier scenario, when you positioned yourself against your manager. You need to have your manager involved and on your side. Then you become intentional cocreators working for the same result.

Managing expectations allows those above you to maneu-ver so they aren't in a bad position if things go wrong. That is the key to managing expectations. Your career is based a lot on not only what you do, but also how you do it. Managing expectations is a way to ensure you're painted in the best possible light with your manager and those involved in your project or impacted by your project.

It's a lot easier for your manager to forgive you for being late on a project due to an unforeseen problem when you informed him or her about the problem immediately, rather than waiting to tell them you will be late when the project was due. Remember, not only is your manager counting on you to deliver, but your company may be counting on you to deliver as well; your project may be factored into month- or year-end financials, and now those are disrupted.

Communication is the key. Managing expectations is also a way to show that you're conscientious enough to inform those around you of the important aspects of your project in case they're asked by their managers. It also creates a reputa-tion of confidence for you, that you are on top of things and have things under control. This translates into dependability, which is like gold in a stressful business or high-demand cul-ture. See how describing the different communication per-spectives breaks down into positive or negative perception? Not communicating well and not managing expectations creates a negative relationship. Communicating and manag-ing expectations fosters a positive environment in which to work—one that's so much easier to function within than a negative environment.

3

Don't Agree to Do What You Don't Want to Do

EARLY IN MY career, I worked at a manufacturing company as a tool and die apprentice; I also supported manufacturing. The president of the company was a clean fanatic. Even in the machine shop, we had to mop the floors and wipe down all the equipment. It was a pain, but it was nice to work in a clean environment. Typically, a coworker and I would clean the manufacturing area as well, sweeping the floor and dusting the manufacturing machines. One day, the president of the company came up to us and asked if we could please come in on Sunday to clean. I said no, that I had things to do. I was young then and worked a lot of hours, and all I really wanted was a day to relax. My coworker was on the fence. The president needed both of us, not just one person, so he pleaded with us, "Please do this for me. I will only ask this of you this one time, as I really need it done." We reluctantly

agreed. He went away happy, and that Sunday I spent cleaning the manufacturing area as the dutiful employee that I
was. Yeah, right.

I was not happy, but I figured, heck, it was only this one
time, and it looked good to help out the boss. Brownie points,
right? Well, you guessed it. Several weeks later, the president
came up to us again and asked us to work Sunday. I said, "No,
I really do not do Sundays, but thanks."

The president replied, "What do you mean you do not do
Sundays? You worked for me on Sunday a few weeks ago, so
you *do* work Sundays, and I need you to help me out again and
work this Sunday."

See what happened? I thought it was one time and I was
doing the boss a favor, but it ended up being an ongoing oc-
currence. I had given up my leverage. I caved into "looking
good to the boss," "feeling sorry for the boss," and to an
empty promise that it was "just this one time."

Lesson learned? You bet. I promised myself I would never
let that happen again. If you do *not* want to do something,
set your boundary, draw the line, and hold to your position.
Management may not like your answer, but that is their problem, not yours.

Now let's move forward. A number of years later, I was
working for a very large company where we were developing a
manufacturing method using new technology for a key product component. I was part of the team focusing on developing
the new technology and the new machine by being hands-on
with manufacturing. That meant I ran the machine, making
preliminary production while tweaking the process to optimize it as much as possible. We were under a lot of pressure to
start full-on production, and time was running short. One day,
one of the managers came up to us manufacturing engineers

and asked us if we would consider working under a new and novel work structure.

We were a very open and innovative plant, so of course, we all said, "Sure, let's hear it." He explained that we would work ten-hour days for four days in a row and get three days off. We asked about holidays and weekends. The manager looked at us, paused, and said, "You don't get any. You're getting three days off a week. How can that be any better?"

I replied, "If this is so good a working system, why is it not the standard for a typical week in the United States?"

"C'mon. Just try it and see," he said. "I think you'll like it. It will be great for you, and you get an extra day off a week."

I thought back to the time at the manufacturing company and the request to work Sunday. I smelled something not quite right, and I had learned my lesson. "I don't think so. If it were that good, it would already be in place. No thanks, I'll pass." The manager continued to plead with me, but he soon realized that I was not budging.

He managed to get the second shift to go to the new system. After several months, they stopped the experiment. I asked them how it was. They replied that it was hell. Sleep deprivation was a problem; they were falling asleep driving home. They missed family events due to the schedule. They told me they sometimes had no idea what day it was. It played havoc with their family life as well. "You were the smart ones by not agreeing to it. I wished I had said no," one of them replied. I felt good and relieved. My lesson from the manufacturing company had paid off. Learn these life lessons, but more importantly, do not forget them. You may change companies, but human nature is the same everywhere.

4

Resolve the Unresolved

HAVE YOU EVER had a puppy? They are adorable, aren't they? But puppies are a handful with training, and they crave and need so much attention. One of the more unpleasant things about puppies is having to house-train them. Oh, it's not pleasant when they have an accident. Not fun at all. Doesn't it seem like if they have a choice between tile and carpet, they always choose the carpet? Ugh. What do you usually do when this happens, besides clean up the accident? You typically find an appropriate way to discipline the puppies to teach them not to do that again. What you're trying to do is teach the puppy the correct behavior. By addressing the issue immediately, you're reinforcing this association. We know that this juxtaposition of consequence to action works to eliminate the problem. If left unchecked, the puppies assume nothing is wrong and maintain the prevailing behavior, having accidents in the house. This is not an ideal situation, of course. But when you immediately correct the puppies, they learn to associate what they did with what you want them to do.

Now, what would you think would be the case if you didn't discipline the puppy when the accident occurred? What if you waited several months, and then one day you just up and disciplined the puppy? What do you think the puppy would do? He or she would more than likely look at you and give you a "what the heck was that for?" look. The puppy would not understand the discipline versus the action. What the puppy would be experiencing is the disconnect between behavior and reaction. There's a lack of association between the two. The puppy wouldn't really get the hint that having an accident in the house was a no-no.

Now apply this to work. Say you did something that someone didn't like, and in keeping with typical human nature, he or she told everyone but you. You heard rumors circulating that someone wasn't happy with what you did. Others added to the rumors, embellishing them, escalating the conflict. The rumors soon have a life of their own. You and the other person don't get along, you both are at odds, and you're not talking to each other. Of course, others enjoy this and add fuel to the fire because they may benefit from the conflict. But is there really a conflict? Do you believe the rumors? Are you convinced the other person truly doesn't like you? You become mad and upset. Both you and the other person talk to your friends, complaining about each other. So what may have started as an innocent comment becomes a full-blown conflict between the two of you.

Why didn't you just talk to the other person and discuss the matter? Because it's easier to complain to someone else—less conflict, less stress. Why do we do this? Why do we tell everyone else but the person who is the source of the conflict?

Isn't this the same as not disciplining the puppy when he or she has an accident? Life would be so much simpler if we all just had honest, constructive dialogue with whomever we have conflict with. That's the same as disciplining the puppy when he or she has an accident, isn't it?

Stop and think—we all do this. We all avoid direct confrontation. We tell our friends we're annoyed by so-and-so, and why didn't so-and-so do this or that? That's the problem with us—we're more comfortable talking to someone we trust, someone we can predict the reaction of and justify our actions through our friend's agreement. That's so much easier than dealing with the problem head-on, isn't it? Doesn't that resolve the problem before it gets out of hand? No, it doesn't. You're fooled if you think otherwise. We all typically avoid confrontation. But we're really creating an enormous amount of stress and anxiety for ourselves with this approach. Initially, it does take a bit more effort, but in the end, direct confrontation is the far better way to resolve conflict.

Confrontation doesn't mean fisticuffs or shouting. It means sitting down in a neutral place and discussing the issue objectively without attacking other people. Try this: Set up a meeting in a quiet, neutral area, and start by asking those involved what their concern was with the issue and the reasoning for what they did. First, try to understand their side, and then you can explain your side. More often than not, you will find that the issue was not as dramatic as you thought, not as grave as imagined, and typically, it was really a misunderstanding. In the end, you may have strengthened your relationship with them, maybe earned their respect, and maybe gained future allies. The right way is often the hard way, but it's always the easiest way in the end. Why is it difficult initially, though? Because we need to swallow our pride. Because we must confront our own feelings and thoughts. We do not like—and have trouble accepting—criticism. This is often challenging for us because we are afraid that, in delving into our motivations and intent, we may be found wrong. Oh my, forbid we make a mistake and are wrong, right?

We are never comfortable admitting we may be wrong. We aren't comfortable discussing our feelings unless we do so with someone we feel agrees with us. It's difficult and awkward confronting someone who disagrees with us. However, we should strive to do it. After a while. it will become easier, and you'll gain the respect of your coworkers as someone who's open and honest. You may think this is the wrong thing to do if you're trying to control perception. Sure, it could have an impact, but I'm pretty sure the perception would be temporary since people will see your integrity as an outcome. What a great way to boost your reputation in the long run.

5

Reality

ONE OF THE hardest things to get across to people is the need to treat everyone with respect and courtesy. The cleaners, the dockworkers—all are filling an important role for the company. Never belittle someone else's job until you have done it as well. Even then, don't do it! It's not good karma. It hearkens to the old adage "Walk a mile in my shoes before you judge me."

I worked at a family-owned business where we converted PVC film. The manufacturing process generated huge boxes of waste material. At the time, I managed a modest maintenance shop as part of my responsibilities. I was walking through the plant with some of the mechanics to look at a job on the manufacturing floor when one of the cleanup workers accidentally knocked over a large scrap box. Ground PVC flakes went all over the floor. The mechanics I was with pointed at what happened and laughed at the guy. They thoroughly enjoyed the scene.

While they were laughing, I went over to the guy, grabbed

a broom lying nearby, and started helping him clean up the mess. After a moment, the mechanics stopped laughing, clearly feeling a bit awkward watching me (their boss) helping while they just stood there. Slowly, one by one, they came over and helped. In a few minutes, the mess was cleaned up. The floor worker thanked us. I told him, "No problem. We are all in this together." From that moment on, whenever I needed something, that floor worker was my best buddy.

After the incident, the mechanics and I eventually made it back to the shop. One of them asked me why I helped the guy—after all, it was *his* job. I replied that I respected the floor worker, as he was doing whatever he could to feed his family and should be respected for that. After all, he was making it a clean, safe place to work.

From that time on, the mechanics had a more helpful attitude and assisted when they saw a need. For my part, I supported them in this action. Because of the mechanics' new attitudes in helping others, over time, work orders decreased, which was a nice but nonobvious outcome. Workers had been putting in work orders just to bother the maintenance shop; such was their reputation over the years. I had a lot to deal with when I took over the department. Well, because of this new teamwork atmosphere, the workers viewed the maintenance shop as a partner, even helping with suggestions for repairs and other issues. The maintenance shop had it easier, and the workers were happier. Because there were fewer work orders, they were completed within hours, if not sooner. The benefit of respect and cooperation that transpired was truly a win-win situation.

A parallel to this scenario was another incident that occurred. At the company, there was a minimum-wage worker who I heard had just bought his first car. He had been in and out of trouble and was really trying to turn himself around. I went up to him, congratulated him, and asked to see his car. He was shocked. "Really?" he said. "You want to see it? Uh, okay, sure."

We went out to the parking lot, and there was his car. It was a ten-year-old car with more paint colors than a paint store. I wondered if it would even run. I hesitated a second, then said to him, "Well, show me around the car." He eagerly showed me its features via a running commentary. He was genuinely proud of the car. Did I need to do this? No, I didn't, but for this guy, the car represented a milestone in his life. He didn't see a multicolored car or a worn, tired vehicle. He saw freedom, the ability to get to work without worrying how, the ability to be independent. He was providing for his family as a good hus-band and father. The ability to purchase it was an achievement in his eyes. I shook his hand and told him he should be very proud of his purchase and wished him good luck with the car.

I will never forget how proud he was. It was moving for me to see how much he relished recognition by someone else for what he did. My acknowledgment meant a lot to him, even if he didn't say so. Did it cost me anything to do that? To recognize someone not as fortunate as me who was do-ing what he could to provide for his family? No, it did not. Afterward, I could always count on him if I needed something done. I was all right in his eyes for a manager. The simple act of showing respect and care created a lasting bond between us. I was the first boss who treated him in this manner, who genuinely showed an interest in him. Hopefully, it made a lasting difference.

At my current job, I know the names of the shipping department workers and the names of the people who empty the trash cans and water our plants. I know the names of those who work in our cafeteria, and I always say hi to them, even when I'm with others. I inquire about their families, what they did for vacation, and so on. They appreciate it as well.

There's a benefit to this. The "little people" can make your life easy or hard. A manager I once had complained that he had been trying for weeks to get a crate moved over to our building from the shipping dock. Our building was located across the parking lot from shipping. I asked him what the matter was. "I do not know," he said. "I have been asking them, yelling at them, threatening them, and arguing with them that I need the crate now, and they still haven't brought it over."

"How long has this been going on?" I asked.

"Two weeks," he replied.

I smiled. "Want me to take care of it for you?"

He shrugged. "Give it a try, but you'll not get anywhere with them. They don't listen. I'm going to inform their manager if they don't get that box over here."

I made a call to the shipping department. Now, I knew everyone there, remember?

Literally a half hour later, I knocked on my manager's door. "Your crate is here."

He was speechless. Once he regained his composure, he asked, "How did you get it over here so fast? I've been trying for weeks!"

"Nothing special," I answered. "I told them I needed it, and they brought it over."

What *really* happened, though? I called over and asked about the crate. They told me my manager could go to hell before they would bring it over. He was a jerk, and he had no business yelling at them. See, they were union, so he couldn't really force them to do anything. "You want it, Eric?" asked the shipping department head.

"Yes, I would appreciate it if you could bring it over."

"Okay, we'll do it for you, but not for that jerk."

Actually, they used much stronger language. (My then manager had a way of ensuring people knew the first moment they met him that he was someone to avoid.)

I got it done because I got to know the people in shipping, and I didn't treat them as a subclass of workers. You catch more bees with honey than you do with vinegar. Is it really that hard to follow the golden rule and treat others as you want to be treated? The simplest effort yields the greatest rewards. I hope you can remember this and apply it in every aspect of your career. Demonstrating a little kindness and respect won't hurt you.

Remember that you and your actions also reflect on your manager and your department. Try to conduct yourself so your department is always viewed in a positive manner. When you take good care of yourself, you also eliminate the need for your manager to deal with petty personality conflicts, which no manager needs to deal with. This makes your manager happy. This is a good thing, since, after all, your manager is a key to your success.

6

Attack the Issue, Not the Person

PEOPLE CAN BE obnoxious, but that's no excuse to lower yourself down to their level, where they may know the rules better than you.

You need to avoid personal conflicts. One should never attack the person. Let's say you're in a meeting and just put forward a proposal that you felt was sound and beneficial. Then someone in the meeting retorts that your proposal is ridiculous. What's your first reaction? You want to defend yourself, right? If the same person said, "I have some questions on your proposal I would like to discuss, as I have a different perspective," what would be your reaction then? Most likely you would say, "Okay, what are they? Let's hear your thoughts, and we can review them to see if they have merit," or something to that effect.

When you say something derogatory to people—attacking

the person—anyone would feel compelled to defend themselves. They are forced to focus on saving face or proving they are right and the accuser is wrong, regardless of what makes sense or what is best for the company. You also put yourself in a very negative light and don't come across as professional.

You may have also created an enemy or an opposition, and that can have disastrous consequences later in your career, especially if the person becomes a manager—or worse, your boss. Then how good would it feel to have called that idea ridiculous?

Always try to keep things professional. Sometimes people have different information or different priorities that make what you want to do not as important as you think. It's always best to keep an open mind—*do not take things personally*—and try to understand what the real issue is. Often, there is an underlying issue they're trying to address, but they don't know it themselves. You end up with a future ally and a professional reputation; and maybe you took a difficult issue and found an easy common ground that all can live with.

Try to keep your emotions in check and give the other person the benefit of the doubt. I know we are all human, and sometimes you just want to reach across the table and use your light saber (oh, how many times …) to make your point, but shut it off and put it back in its holster. Let the person show everyone that he or she is the one acting unprofessionally, the one being rude and inconsiderate.

In meetings, try first to understand what others want to do (and why) before presenting your idea. Going about it that way, you can gain some insight, which may help you when you present your idea and make your arguments. In the long run, this behavior may give you leverage and a much-needed advantage. After all, information is power.

7

Appearances

ONE THING THAT never hurts is to dress the part. Dirty nails, wrinkled shirt, scuffed-up shoes? You really think they're visible attributes your company would want in a manager or high-performing associate? Pay attention to the little things in your dress because others are. You think not? Have you ever heard someone comment on how nice someone's clothes are or how great a person looks in a new hairstyle? And that's just from those who choose to say something. Others quietly notice things and say nothing, especially if they don't know the person. Therefore, first impressions *do* say a lot and have a large impact on how we perceive others.

Remember that you're presenting a complete package to others (what you say, how you act, how you look, and how you comport yourself). Consider your personal hygiene and your breath, especially after lunch. On the other hand, you need not announce your presence long before you arrive or long after you've left, so ease up on the cologne/perfume, please!

Note that some people are allergic to cologne/perfume or it causes them headaches. Another reason not to douse yourself. Just saying.

Yeah, I know, I sound like one of your parents, but this is based on my experience, and I'm trying to help you see those nonobvious things that can trip you up and hold you back without your realizing it. Often the little things create an issue, and the accumulation of these can become a larger problem for you.

8

Eating an Elephant

EVER HEAR THE expression "How do you eat an elephant? One bite at a time." It's very apropos when it comes to projects, especially when your manager dumps something on you that you have no idea how to begin. You must eat an elephant (complete a project) by the end of the month. What would you do? Wait until the last few days and then start eating (working on the project)? Not eat at all? Hope the elephant would go away (project gets reassigned)? Or sit there and lament to anyone within earshot how you're overworked, the job is unfair, you don't have resources to eat the elephant (work on the project). This is often referred to as victim thinking.

Victim thinking is exactly what it says: you are a victim of circumstances, woe is me, nothing I can do about it. It's when people blame their circumstances for their present situation because "it's not my fault, I did not/could not [insert excuse here]." The sad thing is that victim thinking works these days because it seems there's very little in the way of accountability.

Often when you're asked to eat an elephant, you procrastinate. *Stop the victim thinking.* Instead of taking the attitude of "woe is me," I suggest looking at it as a challenge or a way to grow and learn. I'm not going to know everything about everything, but I do know people around me who do. So ask questions! Asking questions will not hurt. No one will think you're stupid. It's better to ask, learn, and digest what you're told than stumble through something and get it wrong. Or, even worse, get it right by dumb luck and never know why it worked. The odds are, the next time you'll get it wrong and will be puzzled as to why.

What's the best way to tackle a job that seems overwhelming and beyond your comprehension? You tackle it piece by piece (one bite at a time) by breaking it down into small steps. Look at the project. There must be something in it about which you have some knowledge. It may be graphics, logistics, chemical, mechanical—anything! Find that *one thing* and break it down as to how you would address it. Now, you know you're dreading doing this job, so you'll want to procrastinate, but you cannot. Instead, spend fifteen minutes working on the aspect of which you have a basic understanding, and then put the project aside. Come back to it later in the day or the next day. The key is to work on the project (eat the elephant) a little each day. Before you know it, you've made strides, and the project doesn't look so bad now, does it?

I've found this to be the best way to get something done that I dreaded doing. Attack it a little at a time. Look, if you spent a half hour on it each day, at the end of a week, you would have spent two and a half hours, and did it kill you? No. Was it painful? No. Did you learn something? Sure. If it's about your technical abilities or about a person's skill, at least you learned you could do more than you thought you could.

If you plan right, you can get the project completed (eat the elephant). Working on the project each day at a planned pace, before you know it, the deadline will arrive, and you're gobbling down your last bite. That's called *planning*, and *that's* called owning the task.

With any project, the effective way to handle any task—simple or complex—is to start as soon as possible and mentally figure out how much time you can devote to eating (working) each day. Maybe figure out how much the elephant weighs (how big in scope the project is), how many days until the deadline, and what that means in terms of what you need to eat (accomplish) every day.

Remember that every problem is surmountable and doable. You just need to break it down to as small a step as possible, and then it becomes manageable. That is the key. Make the project manageable for you and your abilities.

I've found this to be the most effective way to handle many projects. Have you ever seen someone on TV who has all these plates spinning on the end of sticks? They run back and forth between the sticks, keeping the plates spinning. It's a bit of work, but they can accomplish a lot with minimal exasperation. Your knowledge and skills are what limit how many plates (projects) you can keep spinning simultaneously.

Here is an example of how this worked for me. I transferred to a new department within the company where everything was new to me. I was nervous and, quite frankly, scared. I was given ten projects to do on subjects I never handled before. My first reaction was to panic, convince myself that I could never complete the projects. I felt sure I was going to fail. I spent a whole day working on just one project trying to figure out what I had to do and was ignoring my other projects.

The third day of this, I said to myself that working on one project at a time was not going to get my assignments completed. I figured there had to be some way I could take a small portion of a project, something that I was familiar with, and work on that section until I came to a point where I could break off and pick it up again later. After a while I had that section worked out, and I felt good. Maybe this was not a bad idea. I repeated this approach with each of my projects. Soon I was making headway, and things were becoming clearer as to what needed to be done. After a few weeks, I had a project done. Wow! Where I thought I had no possible way to complete all my projects, by breaking them down into small, manageable blocks, I was able to successfully complete my projects on time.

By spending a set time on each project every business day, you can accomplish a great deal. C'mon, try it for a month. First, track your time for a month while you are working. Then try what I described above for a month. Spend a portion of your day working on each of your projects. Compare the results. If you commit to this method, I'm confident you'll be pleased with the results.

9

Contractor, Anyone?

I'VE BEEN WORKING for a long time, and I've seen a lot of flavor-of-the-month concepts, ideas, and programs come and go. What tends to be a growing trend by companies that is here to stay is the hiring of contractors to reduce overhead in terms of salaries and benefits.

So what about contactors? You need to realize that you're a contractor yourself, even if you're a full-time employee. Companies no longer view employees as long-term investments. Why have a full-time employee when I can hire a contractor for less money? A company does not have to pay benefits, companies can release contractors when they're no longer needed, and companies can write off the cost of contractors, unlike a full-time employee who is carried on the books as overhead.

These then are the conditions you'll be working in, the environment to muscle your way through. This means you're competing with contractors for that coveted job.

If you're a full-time employee, consider yourself lucky,

but don't get content. You need to think as a contractor. If you didn't have a job tomorrow, what qualifications would your company be looking for? Remember that companies are hiring very qualified people from outside the United States or contracting companies overseas that command a lower salary than a US worker or US company. This makes them very enticing to a company. What do you need to do to make a company want to hire you?

The worldwide competition for positions is what you're up against. Think long about what a company needs and what you would bring to the table. How can you differentiate yourself from others with the same degree but demanding less in salary? Look to certifications, language skills, diversified positions within your field of expertise, increasing levels of responsibility, your network, publications, patents, or years of experience.

You need to find a way to set yourself apart and sell yourself as a useful investment for the company. Remember that this is a competition, and the gloves need to come off. Be professionally ruthless in your pursuit of a position. You're selling yourself as a resource. What's in it for the company to hire you and not someone who will cost them less?

10

Life 101

YOU'VE PROBABLY NOTICED that each section I've written about covers an aspect of life as it plays out in front of you or as you interact with others. The reality of work in the end is that it's work. It's not your life. It's a means to live; it's not the reason for living. If you're fortunate enough to have a job such as a professional baseball player, then you're in that rarified stratum where your job is not a job. Like anything, there are exceptions.

What I really want you to realize is that you have one life to live. It is up to you how you live that life. Do you really want to spend most of it being miserable? Stressed due to deadlines? Losing or gaining weight from worrying? Suffering from anxiety because you're afraid to lose your job? No one should have to be in a situation where their employment is a sword of Damocles over their head. You need to find a job/career where you enjoy the challenges you're faced with. Keep in mind that the people you work with are as important as the job. The synergy and the companionship you have with your coworkers are just as important as the work itself. If your stress is related to personality conflicts or you work with immature individuals, then this is reason enough to find another job with an atmosphere in which you can flourish.

Realize that your well-being is more important than the money you make or the work you do. You may think differently, especially if you're early in your career. That is because your physical being is very resilient (this, of course, varies by individual) when you are young. But as you age, this becomes more of an issue. Your body can only handle so much stress before it needs to find a way to let you know and to release the stress. The stress can be in the form of muscle tightness, headaches, fatigue, and other challenges to your overall health.

Please hear me on this: if you're stressed and cannot find a solution, you need to find a different job or career. It is not all about the money. All the money in the world cannot cure all ailments of the body, or we would all never die. Stress accelerates aging (gray hair, for example), reduces your energy, and compromises your immune system.

Figure out what you want to get out of life and what you want to accomplish in your career. You shouldn't have to endure undue stress to pursue these goals. This is where Forrest Gump was right: life is like a box of chocolates. You do need to try things to figure out where your passion lies and what gets you up in the morning. The earlier in your life you challenge yourself, the better you'll be in determining what you want to do for a living. If you have a passion you're working at and work with good people, then your life and your job will be a reward in and of itself.

Your goal should be to find a job that doesn't feel like

a job, but something that comes naturally to you. Find the company that has the right people and fulfills your passion; then you will be truly living a full life of vigor and rewards.

Your Career Begins

One thing that's hard for graduates to understand is the need to minimize your debt and not to grow your debt. Of course, you have school loans, but do you need that high-end car, the latest phone, dinner at that new upscale seventy-five-dollar-a-plate restaurant? There's a difference between things we need and things we desire. Believe me, if you manage your debt and only buy what you can afford, then you will be able to have financial freedom later on in life. Life is a balance between now and the future. Why bury yourself in debt? Your job suddenly becomes a must. You lose career flexibility, and you stress over being laid off or fired. You need this job; you need the money, or how else can you pay your bills? Really? Do you need to send your kids to that expensive private school because everyone else is? Do you need to pay for horse-riding lessons? Face reality. Live within your means. Better yet, live slightly below the standard you desire and use the difference to pay down your school loans. There are a lot of activities that don't cost anything, like museums, parks, historical sites, public concerts, hiking, bicycling, picnicking, reading, tennis, basketball, the beach, and so on. These don't cost anything, and the best part is they are socially interactive activities that don't involve the internet or television.

My wife and I had barely any money starting out. We developed a budget to pay off school loans. We only had one credit card, and we only charged what we could pay off at the end of the month. If we couldn't pay it off, we would wait and save the money until we had enough and then buy it on credit and pay the card at the end of the month with the savings. If you cannot afford something, how can you afford to pay high interest rates? In this manner, my wife and I were able to pay off our loans and pay off our mortgage before our children were of college age. This gave us the financial freedom to pay for our children's college without taking out loans! We planned for events and stayed within our financial means. Now we do whatever we like—dine out, take trips, and buy what we need without worrying.

Having this financial freedom allows us to live our lives on our terms, not someone else's. We aren't worrying about our jobs because we have the financial flexibility to work within a wide salary range. The job then is no longer important to us because we are not slaves to the income.

This can get complicated, but the lesson I'm trying to convey is to keep your expenses slightly below your means, pay yourself first, pay down your loans, put money aside for savings (IRAs, ROTH, etc.), and then pay your bills. You will never get ahead if you don't take care of yourself first. Doing this ends up making the job less important, as you have built in the financial flexibility you need, and you can enjoy life on your terms, not your manager's. Get rid of the sword of Damocles!

11

Think Like a Manager

IF YOU WISH to be a manager, think like one and act like one. That does not mean going around bossing everyone. If you do, you misunderstand how managers should comport themselves. What do I mean by acting like a manager? Managers are supposed to be people who see the big picture, treat others with respect, are informed, and own their responsibilities. They are supposed to help their workers in their careers, defend them to those outside of their department, and acts as their mentor. Yes, managers are supposed to also help their workers accomplish their objectives by helping them overcome obstacles in their way. Here is a story that may help you understand how a manager can support you in your work.

I started working for a large company in Pennsylvania that was designed to enable engineers to work running production as they developed a new technology for making a surgical component. The work was cutting edge for its time and relied heavily on old and emerging technology. My job was to work on fine-tuning the equipment for full-scale production. It was a novel work environment since we were engineers running production—not a common theme in the late eighties. Also, we were flat—no hierarchy. The whole place was team-oriented. We could talk to anyone at any time. A very refreshing way to work.

I had several managers while there. There were power struggles that took place that ended up reshuffling managers. After the dust settled, I ended up getting a new manager. He was very good, very smart, but very demanding. I got along well with him, and we made many improvements and had many successes. My fellow engineers and I were on a roll. We were truly functioning as a team, each supporting the other and making huge strides toward our overall goals.

One day, a new hire started, and things changed immediately. From functioning as a team, we immediately went to a me-first atmosphere. Those who had been there continued to try working as a team, but every time the new hire got involved, the whole team concept of working together flew out the window. He was a very me-first person. In fact, one of the engineers told him to his face that he would sell his mother if he could make a dollar. He just smiled at her and walked away.

Soon the new guy was hanging around with my manager—going to lunch and successfully lobbying for assignments that took him away from having to operate production equipment. I was getting frustrated because he wasn't pulling his weight. I figured my work would speak for itself, so I put my head down and did my job. I figured it was typical office politics, and eventually things would work themselves out. Others saw what was happening; people within and outside of our department were surprised at how I was being treated.

Eventually, my manager started taking various jobs from

me to give to the new guy. I asked why, but I never got a straight answer. Basically, the new guy was convincing my manager that he should be the lead engineer, not me. I should have been less naïve. I got frustrated and started looking for opportunities at other company locations. Eventually, I found a job in technical services at another site and left. After I held this position for more than a year, the company decided to dissolve the technical services department, so I ended up in research and development.

After some time in my new position, there was a reorganization of research and development that resulted in my getting a new manager—my former manager from Pennsylvania, the same manager who had given me grief! Crap! A fellow worker heard the news and said he was getting out; he didn't want to work for the manager and said I should do the same. The manager didn't have a good reputation. Demanding and very accountable, he wasn't easy to work for. I understood why my coworker wanted to leave, but I felt I needed to see if I could learn to work with him in a different role. As I said, he was demanding, but he was smart and had taught me a lot. I thought that without the guy around who drove me out of Pennsylvania, I could make a go of it, and maybe the situation would be different. I also felt one should not run away from one's problems. There comes a time when you need to face them and see what the lesson is you need to learn.

Soon, the manager transition took place. Yes, he was still the same difficult manager to work with. He didn't let you get away with anything. However, I sensed he was trying to make things work.

Working for him wasn't so bad. I was glad I didn't leave. One day, he gave me a small project that was very complicated but doable. I spent several weeks on it until it took me to a point where I had two options and wasn't sure which to take. I figured, what the heck, I'll ask my manager what he wants me to do.

This is where I learned a very good lesson from him. I presented the issue and said, "Well, what do you want me to do?"

My manager said, "You want me to do your job for you and figure out what to do? That's your job. You should come to me with your options, the pros and cons, and your recommendations. Then I can review and agree or not. But to come to me and ask what to do without your doing any background work to understand the options is a weak position to take. You will never learn how to make decisions if you always rely on others to make them for you."

That was a heavy response, but as I walked back to my office with my tail between my legs, I thought about what he'd said. And it made sense. I was relying on him to make a decision; I was avoiding making one. I went back to my desk and worked out each option, weighed the different options, and came back to my manager with my recommendation. He agreed with my conclusions, and I moved forward with the project accordingly.

I learned from this that you do need to think like the manager at times. Look at what the options are and what could be the pros and cons of either direction, and then weigh the options against different factors. This puts you in a better position with your manager and shows you're thinking of the needs from a big-picture perspective as well as a practical perspective.

Think like a manager and figure out what to do and why. This is the way to learn how to be a manager.

Later, I would take this approach and think through decisions that had to be made. I also studied my manager's decisions and style to learn what he looked for in things. This made my decisions better.

At some point a few years later, my manager was moving on to a new position. One day, he pulled me aside and thanked me. I asked him what for, and he said I had done a lot to help him and make him look good as a manager. He was being observed to see how he would work as a manager. I had helped make him look successful, hence, the thanks. I later found out that management knew about his performance when I'd worked with him before, and they were watching to see if he'd changed.

It was a win-win all around for both my manager and me in learning new perspectives and gaining confidence and responsibility.

As a manager, do not allow people to go to you without first going through your direct reports. People need to respect those who work for you. Make sure they work out a solution with your direct report before you get involved. If you don't ensure this behavior, then your direct reports will not have the respect they deserve, and you, the manager, will end up doing their work for them by making the decisions.

It's my opinion that managers should learn about their direct reports. Learn about their background, what they like to do, and what they don't like to do. What are their aspirations, and what do they think about their projects? The more you learn and understand what makes your direct reports tick, the better you can formulate career options for them and guide them toward successful outcomes.

One thing I learned as a manager is not to treat every direct report the same. Each person has different strengths and weaknesses. Some are good at handling multiple projects; others are not. Good managers tailor the work and amount of work according to the skills and abilities of each person who reports to them. If you have people who are very detail-oriented, it may not be a good idea to load them up with multiple projects—they just don't function well like that. They may be better suited to a single, complex project, where they can thrive. Using this approach, you will find that you can optimize your resources and more efficiently handle issues and control project timing for your department.

As a manager, the success of the people who work for you is your success. You are there not only to get projects completed, but also to grow the future human resources of your company.

12

You at Work

CONGRATULATIONS! YOU HAVE a job! For some of you, it may be a compromise, so you *have* a job, anything to start paying off those annoying student loans. For others, it took a lot of networking, and sure, it is a low-level position, but you have your foot in the door. Then there are others who, no matter what they do, always seem to get the cherry job with the ridiculous salary and benefits. Yes, there are all kinds of people in the world, and you will meet all kinds on the job. Get used to it; that's reality. You will meet people who have no clue what they are doing and are always screwing up, but their manager just *loves* them! You stop and wonder, "Are they seeing the same thing I see?"

Then there are those who seem to be lost in a world of their own. They just sit at their desk and crunch numbers and bang out charts and analyses that no one really understands or sees how the information has any benefit to them or the business. And you have the social butterfly, who flits from one cubicle to the next, talking about themselves ad nauseam, or better yet, did you hear the latest gossip … who got fired, promoted, yelled at, hurt, who is having an affair and so on. Or here's the best one—how busy they are. If they're so busy, why are they here talking to me and everyone else? Yes, people do need a break at times to refresh themselves from concentrating and it *is* a way to maintain a network; however, they should be more mindful of others and their time.

There are people who, when asked to do something, respond, "Sorry, no way. I'm too busy to do that." Or they reply, "You need to talk to my boss to get approval for me to work on that." This is deflection. It's a stalling technique because it forces you to go through the system to get them to work on something. How do people get away with this? Blame their manager.

I could go on and on with examples, but generally, there are people who lie low and do the work in silence, those who do minimal work but do a very effective job of appearing to be busy, and the most dangerous of all, those who gossip and avoid work through their network.

Yes, it's the subtle ones who are the most dangerous. Be aware and be diligent. The more you know whom you're really dealing with and what their motivation is, the better your chances of survival.

Sure, you can be really good at what you do, and that alone will lend a degree of job security, but in the end, that may not be enough to get a promotion. It may come down to making an ultimatum to your boss. Sometimes people do not get a promotion because management knows the job is essential to their financial well-being. Did they not tell Sally at lunch that they have

- a huge mortgage;
- mounting medical bills;
- suffocating school loans;
- a wife/husband/partner who is out of work, so they *have* to work; or
- parents in an assisted living center to support?

The thing is, you never want to put yourself in a position where management feels they *own* you. You don't want to lament about the huge bill for college and how you must pay it. Sure, you have a huge bill, but it's better to say, "Yeah, I have this huge college tuition due this month, but we planned for it and are in good shape." Keep these things to yourself. It is best not to say anything. I've worked at places where they threaten to fire you. Yes, there are perverted bosses out there, and I have had my share—no reason to make things worse by making yourself vulnerable to intimidation.

It's a breath of fresh air when you meet people at work and realize they are just like you. You feel normal, not crazy. Then you examine their career and see they aren't going anywhere fast, either. Why? Well, the why has a lot to do with your behavior and attitude.

Think like a movie star and that you're playing a role. Would you rather portray yourself as incompetent, rude, mistake-prone, and stressed out, or as competent, capable, confident, and thorough? Or would you prefer a role where you portray yourself as the complete opposite? There does exist a fine line, and knowing where that line is and how to walk it is a big part of your success. It really comes down to people's impressions of you or *perceptions*.

13

You as a Manager

As a manager, you need to realize that those who report to you are looking to you for protection, career guidance, and aid in personal development. Your job is not to succeed at your direct reports' expense; it's to develop your direct reports. Their success is your success. This seems to be a perspective not realized by a lot of managers. There are a number of key ways managers can support and grow their direct reports.

Good Manager

If something happens that merits recognition, let your direct reports enjoy the recognition. As a manager, take satisfaction that one of your team members did something well. It's not the position of a manager to take credit for the work and efforts of others. Good and effective managers are seemingly behind the scenes, helping their team, working their network to assist their team in accomplishing their goals.

I was handling a workload that was the equivalent of two people's. We had a person in our group retire, and all his work went over to me, along with what I was already handling. We had a lot of base business issues to deal with, so I jumped in with both feet to resolve them. At that time (and still to this day), research and development did not want anything to do with base business. Their job was to think of new things, not fix problems with current designs, even though they owned all product designs. Most of what I did was in support of existing products instead of focusing on new product development. That was because there was a lot of work to be done in support of existing products.

Every week, my manager and I met and reviewed my projects. Never in any weekly meeting did my manager admonish me not to work on base business activities and projects, so I didn't think they were an issue for him. All was good, at least as I could surmise from our meetings. We went through my year's accomplishments one by one, and there were a lot. I handled thirty-eight projects that year in one form or another. All of them were on target or successfully completed.

In the end, my manager said my performance was average. I asked about all the work I did and the successes I had and how I had picked up all the work of the retired engineer. He said that base business didn't matter. Imagine how I felt hearing this and how demotivating it was for me.

As a manager, you need to know what your direct reports are working on, their workload, and the effort they are putting forth. If you're having one-on-ones, that's the time to discuss progress and how your manager is tracking your performance. At the end of the year, your performance rating should be aligned to what was discussed and conveyed during the one-on-ones.

Have conversations with your direct reports on what they want to do with their careers. Learn what they like and dislike. Talk to them and engage them in conversations about their aspirations. Then, as a manager, you can work with them and help them get the training, experience, or position that will help them achieve their goals. I had many such conversations like this with my direct reports. I did not promise them anything, but they saw that I was making an effort. This helped develop a respect and appreciation, which contributed to a great working relationship.

Not-So-Good Manager

Never say that politics or a poor manager does not affect your career. These impacted my ability to get a promotion and affected my earnings. From this I hope you see that it's crucial to your career and personal growth to get a good manager—a damn good one. Sometimes you don't have a choice, but there are always options. Hopefully, you will never have to deal with anything quite like I did but will learn from my experience. You are only as good as your manager's support for you. I repeat: *you are only as good as your manager's support for you*. If your manager is stalling promotions or is full of excuses when you discuss your career, you need to find another job. Too bad if you think it's the perfect job for you; it's not. Sooner or later, you'll find that out, so why waste the years and potential loss of income?

When reading this, if you recognize these traits in your manager, please start working on an exit plan! Here are some danger signs you are working for a poor manager:

- Your manager offers vague reasons why you cannot get promoted.
- Your manager does not help lay out a development plan for you.
- Your manager does not let you participate in growth programs such as rotations or special projects.
- Your manager takes your ideas as his or her own.
- Your manager cannot make time to help you.
- Your manager is overcritical even when you have a success.
- Your manager does not have your back with upper management (this is a huge one!).
- Your manager does not recognize good work or your successes.
- You are not comfortable being around your manager.
- It's your manager's way or no way.
- You do not want to say anything in front of your manager.
- Your manager is condescending and disrespectful to you.
- The quality of your sleep is affected.
- You feel anxious when in conversation with your manager or before you need to meet with him or her.
- You start to feel stressed at work, and work is no longer fun.

You will help your career tremendously if you pay attention to these warning signs. Take control of your career instead of going with the flow. Remember, ultimately it is you who is responsible for your career, not your manager. But a good manager can significantly boost your career and provide valuable insight. A not-so-good manager is not forthcoming with career help and tends to place roadblocks in your way, and that's a good reason not to rely on a bad manager.

14

Presentations

Presentations are tough if you lack confidence or are intimidated by who will be in the audience. This is natural. No one wants to embarrass himself or herself or appear incompetent. Giving presentations and looking comfortable and relaxed takes practice. It comes easier for some than others, but this is due, in part, to people's personalities. I took a class on communications, and over the years, I learned some things that were very helpful. Here are some tips I hope will help you as well.

Setting the Stage

First, if you're giving a presentation to a group of people outside of your company, it's a good idea to dress one level up from them. If it's a business casual meeting, consider a dress shirt and tie. Dressing up a level lends you a degree of formality, authority, and professionalism.

Second, the audience doesn't know what you're going to say. That's why they're there. You could have an entire speech prepared for them, change it on the fly, and no one in the audience would be the wiser. So relax!

Third, practice, practice, practice. The more you understand your material, the easier it will be for you to relax and go with it. A word of caution: do not try to memorize your speech. You could forget a word or lose your place in the speech, and wind up with a blank look on your face with no idea what to say next. You'd get anxious, which makes it worse, and the audience would become uncomfortable because they'd know you were in trouble.

If this happens, take a deep breath, collect your thoughts, and move on. There's one thing you need to realize when giving a speech: the audience does not want to see you fail. Audiences want you to provide them with the information you wish to convey, but they are not there urging you to fail, waiting to pounce on you for the littlest mistake. Audiences are very forgiving. After all, they know what they would be doing in your shoes, and they would want encouragement as well.

Fourth, when you practice, do so in front of a mirror. Better yet, use your smartphone to video your speech. It's a great way to see what you're doing when you're stumbling. Pay particular attention to "ers," "ahs," and "you knows." These are fillers we all have the habit of using because we don't want silence while we're thinking of the next thing to say. We think we need to fill the silence. It's common with everyone, but in a speech, it can become very annoying to constantly hear "you know, you know, you know." Instead, stop! Be quiet! Stop and compose your next thought. When you're ready, continue your speech. Stopping to gather your thoughts is sometimes referred to as a "power pause." The audience is waiting for you to say something, and they have no choice but to wait for you to start talking again. This means you are in control, which is why it's referred to as a power pause.

Gracing the Stage

If you're in a small room—say, a room with fewer than thirty people—and two people start a side conversation, first, realize that it's rude of them, and second, recognize that their conversation is interfering with others who are trying to listen to you. There are two ways to handle the situation. One thing you can do if this is an option for you and you're comfortable doing it is to casually walk around the room. If you're using a fixed microphone, then this is obviously not an option. But if you can, casually walk around the room and make your way to where the side conversation is happening and stand behind the people talking. You'll see how quickly that conversation stops!

If this isn't an option, then another trick is to just stop talking and look at the offending audience members having the side conversation. The audience will pick up on what you're doing, and they, too, will stare at the offenders. It's fun to see how this works. It causes nothing but embarrassment for them. It also serves to enforce the focus on your talk. I have successfully employed this technique. It really works. I can assure you that no one else will talk among themselves after that!

One thing I dislike, absolutely *detest*, is when presenters read their slides. What do I need you for then? Everyone in the room is literate, so why do you feel compelled to read every word on every slide? What you should be doing is allowing the audience to view the slides while you provide color commentary that adds to the information on the slide, that augments the contents by adding examples or additional information. So please, do not read your slides!

If nervousness prompts you to read your slides, then consider the following.

People are visual by nature. We all like to look at things rather than hear a description. When I need to give a speech with slides, I spend a lot of time thinking of the message I'm trying to convey.

For example, say I need to make a presentation on the five food groups: dairy, vegetables, meat, grain, and fruit. Look at the slide below.

FIVE BASIC FOOD GROUPS

GRAIN   bread, cereal
DAIRY   yogurt, milk, butter
MEAT   lamb, beef, fish, pork
FRUIT   oranges, apples, grapefruit, grapes
VEGETABLES   peas, carrots, beets, beans

The slide is all words, and of course, you are going to read every word, because that's the information I wished to convey. Now if I spent a little time, I could figure out a visual way to convey the same information, maybe using a pyramid as in the slide below.

This slide shows the importance of each food group by its position on the pyramid. You can talk about the same information, but look at what you did. You provided your audience with a visual representation of your information, and the visual conveys more information than just the words. The audience will also remember the pyramid a lot longer than a wordy slide. "Oh, hi, you're the person with that food pyramid! I liked your presentation. Thanks for all the good information!" I doubt they would come up to you in the hall and say, "Oh, hi, you're the person who gave that fantastic food speech with those slides with all that information that you read to us! I liked your presentation!" I really, *really* do not think so.

The other benefit of using pictures is that you don't need to spend a lot of time retooling your slides for different audiences. The slides are the slides. All you need to do is alter what you say. See how pictures actually make your presentation so much easier?

The Presentation

With that out of the way, let's talk about how you stand. Look at people on news channels. They look relaxed, and they stand still. Their hands are at their sides, and if they do move them to emphasize a point, it is minimal movement. They don't want to distract the listener with hand gestures. However, this is uncomfortable. Try standing in front of a mirror and start talking with your hands at your sides. How long before you start feeling very awkward and uncomfortable? Not long at all, is it? Of course it's uncomfortable, because it's not natural. One way to compensate for this is to hold your forearms at right angles to your upper arms. This is also a great way to start your presentation. Then as you're talking, just move your forearms slightly up or down or slightly back and forth to the sides. This minimal movement will allow you to feel comfortable and more relaxed, but it doesn't cause a distraction to the audience.

Know your audience. If your presentation is to management, then think strategically in your presentation, because that's management's role—to think strategically. If your audience is comprised of engineers, then your presentation can be technical in nature. But that same presentation to an assembly of office administrators would fall flat. This is not meant to be a slight, but to represent an extreme example. Your job as a presenter is to ensure your audience *understands* what you're trying to convey. A heavily technical discussion to a manufacturing audience would lose them right at the beginning, and they will walk away having learned very little.

While you're presenting, look around the audience. You don't need to make eye contact. That may unnerve you and throw you off. Instead, generally focus on the left side of the room and slowly scan to the right. Then slowly scan back to the left. This does not mean you oscillate like a fan. Stop for a few seconds as you scan, then continue. While doing this, also practice looking at the front of the audience and scan in the same manner to the back of the audience. If you do this, the audience will feel you're engaging them rather than just staring at your notes.

If this is too difficult for you and you must read from your notes, practice reading the beginning of a sentence and speaking the balance of the sentence while looking at the audience. To help your nerves, place a finger in front of your next sentence. This way, when you look back down at your notes, you can find the place where you left off.

A small thing to remember is to empty your pockets. You don't want to be bouncing your knee while standing causing loose change to jangle or be walking around with your hands in your pockets jangling loose change; it's distracting to the audience and a sign of nervousness. For women, remove or avoid loose bracelets that may clang together when you move your arm. This is also distracting to an audience.

Finally, to build up your public speaking confidence, take random topics and write them down on slips of paper. Mix them up in a container. Then reach in and pull out a slip of paper, read the topic, and begin speaking on it for three minutes. Try to avoid those "ers," "ahs," and "you knows" while speaking. This clever technique will build your confidence and help you appear more poised and polished when speaking. It can even help you in speaking extemporaneously.

15

Your Résumé

LIKE MANY OF you, I have interviewed and been interviewed, but still it is amazing to know, with all of the information available on the internet, there are still people who just don't get it. I'm talking about professionals, people who should know better when it comes to interviewing and writing résumés. Here are some dos and don'ts.

Check your spelling and your grammar. Make sure you use a consistent font. A résumé is not a graphic spectacle—you do not need to switch fonts every other sentence. Use fonts and lines to improve the readability of your résumé; excessively varying fonts will not impress the reader. I have even read résumés where sections were cut and pasted from a previous résumé, and all the fonts were different.

Pay attention to the black-and-white spacing of your résumé. This refers to the size of your margins, line spacing, and how the overall page looks. Do not try to cram everything onto a single page. Balance the look of the page and structure the layout so it looks even throughout. Start bullets with action words. Instead of "Responsible for manufacturing specifications," try "Created instructional specifications for manufacturing." Do not state something that is not a fact. I have read many a résumé where the person claimed to be an expert in something, yet when I asked him a very basic question on the subject, he could not provide the correct answer. So above all, be honest. If you didn't do something, then don't state that you did. You will only trip up on your answers in the interview. During questioning, if you're asked if you can do something and you cannot, simply say no but qualify your answer with, "That is something that I feel I can learn given my background and past experiences." Sounds a lot better, doesn't it?

Make sure the job is what you're looking for. I interviewed a potential candidate for a quality hands-on position. The candidate's résumé was impressive. It had everything we were looking for, and he seemed like a good, if not a perfect, fit. We got down to the interview and started asking questions based on the bulleted summaries in his résumé. One bullet stated he had designed a medical component. I asked what and how he carried out the design steps. He replied that he had directed a team to develop the design and oversaw an external design house. Does this sound like he did the actual designing? No, but that's what his résumé said. Think about the disconnect between what he stated he did, versus what he said he actually did. Hopefully this helps you see the bigger picture when interviewing. Make sure you can back up what you state in your résumé.

Try not to get too buzzword-heavy, either. It becomes really obvious that you're trying to impress the reader. Check your dates. If there are gaps between jobs, fill them in or be prepared to explain them. If you're going to write a summary that lays out your career aspirations, make sure it's aligned with the job you're interviewing for. Use nice paper. It doesn't need to be parchment or have a fancy pattern—just good-quality white paper. You don't need to put "References upon request" on your résumé." That's something that's either a company policy or at the discretion of the company's hiring officer. If they want references, they will ask for them. Basically, make sure the résumé spells out exactly what you want to say. Make it positive, sincere, and truthful.

If you're going to state you're an expert on something, I would expect you to have an advanced degree in the subject or be able to provide evidence on what certifies you as an expert. Be very careful saying you're an expert in Windows programs. Just because you can type in Word does not make you an expert. Experts know obscure functions, can do unusual routines in a program, and can explain or demonstrate the skill.

Confirm the location of the interview, as it ensures you will be on time. *Get there early* so you can calm down. Go to the restroom, check your hair, and if applicable, check your makeup. Wash your hands to get off any nervous sweat. Using hot water will also help warm them up so they don't feel cold when shaking hands. Check your clothes. Make sure they are ironed/pressed and clean, and all buttons are there. Take any loose change out of your pockets. This way, if you nervously bounce your leg during the interview (by the way, don't do that!), the interviewer will not hear the jangling change.

Now listen carefully. Take your phone out of your pocket. Shut off the phone. Put the phone in your purse, briefcase, coat pocket, wherever—just not in your pants pocket. You do not want the phone going off during the interview, and please, if your phone does ring, do not answer it. It's unbelievable how many times this has happened during interviews.

When sitting down, sit with your legs together and sit back in the chair but lean slightly forward from the waist. This lends the impression of eagerness to your responses. If you're not sure what to say, say nothing! Wait until you have formulated your response, then reply. This is better than hemming and hawing with "ers" and "ahs" and "you knows" or using any of the other fillers.

Relax … relax … relax … take deep breaths …

Research the company before your interview. With the internet today, there is no excuse for not knowing about a company and its related news.

After you have written your résumé and checked the structure and grammar, have a friend look it over. By the time you are done, you will have looked over your résumé countless times. When that happens, it's easy to miss something. Having a friend look it over is a great way to eliminate errors or mistakes you overlooked.

Try a dry run of the interview with a friend. This is a great way to get comfortable with obvious questions. Your friend can provide valuable feedback on the impression of your answers and how you came across—stiff, nervous, unsure, or otherwise. Do not practice too much. You don't want to be too canned in your answers or come across as overrehearsed. Try videoing yourself using your smartphone. This way, you can see how you look for yourself during specific questions and answers.

Above all, make sure you know what the job is expecting from you. If it involves travel, then make sure you can accommodate travel in your life. If it requires shifts or specific hours, make sure you have a plan for childcare or pet-sitting. And in the end, are you really okay with it all? Ask yourself, "Is this really what I want?"

If you have been in the workforce for a very long time, keep your résumé to the last ten years. You can always provide details prior to this time, but it helps keep your résumé short. Exceptions on this would be if previous jobs had special skills. If so, you can always list them as bullets.

I have read some résumés that shift from first to third person. So my final advice on your résumé is to be sure you maintain the same point of view and maintain parallel syntax.

16

Data

I HAD A great manager once tell me that I could present information that would not be well received by management, and if the information were based on opinion, I would be eaten alive. However, if it were based on data, what could management do? No one likes bad news, and you never want to state a conclusion that's not based on data. If your conclusion is based on data, what can management do? The data is the truth, and management needs to address it. But if you make a statement that doesn't sit well with management and there are no data behind it, well, good luck to you. You probably won't do that more than once. Always have evidence/data to support your conclusions. Without them, you're leaving yourself open to attack. Be smart and be prepared—not defenseless.

Data tell an unassailable story/statement to management. Yes, statistics can say whatever you want (that's another discussion), but data are data. Data are an important tool in diagnosing issues and making a decision. Whenever possible, develop your position from data. You can certainly add opinions based on the data as recommendations, but be sure to preface them as an opinion. For example, "Based on the data and the conclusion that lot A is not the same as lot B, it is my opinion that lot B should be scrapped."

If you only said, "I would scrap lot B," management would ask why.

If you replied, "I think it's a bad lot," then that wouldn't get you far with management. If you based the recommendation on data, then you paint a completely different picture to management. Their decision or agreement to your recommendation is based on data—data they can point at to justify *their* decision to *their* management. Otherwise, what would they say to their management? "Oh, Bob didn't like lot B and wanted it scrapped, so we agreed." Based on what? Bob's opinion?

Data will save your neck. Think about it.

A word of caution about data and statistics. Statistics can be used to say almost anything. A good statistician can manipulate a chart or the way the data are analyzed to get them to imply whatever is desired, so be careful in accepting any statistical analysis without studying the way the data were interpreted. Just as important is knowing how the data were obtained. Statistics are only as good as the integrity of the data. Start with a review on how the data were collected. If data taken from different sources are being compared, be sure the data were collected in the same manner. Are the testing parameters the same? Is the equipment the same? These are important factors to verify.

When I was working in operations, the manufacturing site wanted to change the material supplier. It needed my department's approval to do so. They presented their data, and the quality engineer provided his statistical summary. (I don't want to get into statistics too far, so bear with me on this. And you statisticians out there—please cut me some slack.) Management at that manufacturing site stated that "at a 99 percent confidence level, the material from the two manufacturers is equivalent." Sounds good, right? Wrong. A 99 percent confidence level means you're using a very large confidence interval to capture all possible averages of the material. This is like saying before a horse race that out of nine horses, you can say with a 99 percent confidence that one of the nine horses will be the winner. What rubbish. Of course, it must be one of the nine horses. Stating a 99 percent confidence is basically saying nothing. What the quality engineer should have used, which is common, is a 95 percent confidence level. This would require you, for the hypothetical horse race, to state that the winner would be from one of eight, rather than nine horses. This restricts your ability to state equivalency. The lower the confidence level, the tighter the comparison; the more sensitive the data are to differences. If the material is different and you want to detect a difference, you would want a more restrictive comparison or a tighter confidence level. When the material was compared at a 95 percent confidence level, four out of five of the materials were different. Nice try, manufacturing.

When comparing results from different charts, make sure the scales are the same so you're looking at the charts in the same way.

Another thing to guard against is when something is tested and the response by manufacturing is that the data meet specifications. Check to be sure they have the data to support that acceptable product can be produced at the extremes of the specification. For legacy processes, specifications may have been set without testing to ensure acceptable product can be produced throughout the specification. You can never assume in testing.

17

¿Se Habla Español?

WHEN I WAS growing up, the United States, by and large, was very secular in terms of language. For the most part, you only heard English spoken. If you did hear another language, the chances were it was on television. Over the decades, changes in world dynamics, changes in immigration laws, and changes in immigration tolerance have altered the demographics. Now it seems you cannot go through a day without hearing another language, such as Spanish or Chinese, for example.

Companies have recognized there are new opportunities for growth as new markets develop as countries industrialize or provide enticing tax benefits. Thus, companies establish new operations in foreign countries, which results in the need to translate documents and modify programs to adjust to cultural needs. These changes introduce the need for multilingual workers. As companies become more and more global, the need for multilingual workers will continue to increase.

A great way to springboard your career is to learn another

language. In this global economy, multilingual ability is a golden ticket in a lot of careers. Chinese, Spanish, German, French, Russian, Italian, and Hindi are just a few examples. Having multilingual skills can open positions for you in your company's global operations. If you speak more than one language, your value and opportunities will increase. Multilingual skills will be more and more in demand, so you should give serious consideration to learning another language. Knowing a second or even a third language is a definite plus for your career.

In a company where I worked, Spanish, Chinese, Hindi, German, and French were languages we needed to work with every day. How much easier my job would have been if I could have spoken one of these languages!

18

Door-to-Door Sales, Anyone?

(WELL, THAT'S NOT exactly what I am advocating, but close.)

In today's world, you aren't just competing with others from across the United States but with well-qualified workers from around the world. They have an advantage over us in the United States; they have a desire to work and prosper in America, which makes them very hungry and willing to do whatever it takes. This makes the competition aggressive. To land a good job, you need to sell yourself to prospective companies. You need to stand out and demonstrate that you have unique skills and abilities that place you head and shoulders above any other candidate. Getting a job is really all about differentiating yourself and showing why you are hands down the best person for the job via your skills, ability, and education while using your network.

"Hey, Eric, I'm in school, so how can I develop a network?"

Good question. One excellent way to develop a network is to participate in an intern or co-op program. Schools with such programs, like Drexel in Philadelphia for engineering, help you get your foot in the door. If you play your cards right (think perception here!), you could even convert the experience into a job offer upon graduation. This also may have an advantage in securing a better starting salary. Here's a true story of two interns and what I mean.

Two people were hired to support a major project. They were tasked with processing documentation, obtaining information, and fulfilling general project needs. Both were excellent workers and learned fast. We relied on them a lot as the project progressed. Everyone on the project liked working with them, and the quality of their work was very good. Near the end of the project, they were both going to graduate. Project management really liked them, and so, after some internal discussions, both were offered full-time positions with the company.

(I am going to make up the salaries here, but the differential is real.) The first intern was offered a full-time position with a starting salary of forty thousand dollars. She accepted. The second intern was offered the same position at the same salary but turned it down. The hiring personnel was surprised and asked why. The second intern replied that he wasn't joining the company fresh out of school. He had spent two summers working and learning the company's systems and getting to know employees. He was coming in with a degree of experience and therefore should be offered a higher salary than someone right out of school.

The hiring personnel considered the intern's position and

countered with a salary of fifty thousand dollars. The second intern accepted. That second intern used some very slick thinking. You must admire his thinking and nerve to turn down the initial offer. Of course, this was a large company that had flexibility regarding the salary. But the lesson here is that you can counter any offer if you have a legitimate argument. You do need to be prepared if they say no, but it never hurts to ask.

You can also try asking for an additional week of vacation instead of increased salary; this is often a way to get extra benefits at little cost to the company. It does depend on the company, but you get the idea. Leverage your skills and do not be afraid to ask for what you want.

19

Be Positive

IS THE GLASS half empty or half full? You can make your life more difficult and tedious depending on how you answer this simple question. I have often been in situations where I'm handed an assignment that I absolutely hated and dreaded. I was sure I couldn't do the job and it would end up costing me in my year-end review.

Woe is me.

I found that when I felt like this, the job wouldn't get done or would elicit only a tepid effort on my part, and then it would become a self-fulfilling prophecy—ultimately the job would bring me down in the eyes of my manager.

Negative thinking got me nowhere.

But now, let's take that same task and look at it from a positive perspective. "I don't know what the hell to do, and I don't know how to begin this project; but this is a learning experience, a chance to grow as a person, to learn more about the company/products. Basically, it's a challenge for me to see what I can do." When I looked at the same project from a positive perspective, I felt energized, confident, and excited for the learning experience.

See the difference that attitude makes? It really is that simple—own the task, own your confidence, own your belief in yourself, and the possibilities are enormous. I got the project done; it actually wasn't as hard as I thought it would be. I did learn, I did grow, and my manager was very pleased with what I delivered.

In the end, your attitude and how you face adversity and obstacles put in your way will define your career more than you realize—and define what you are as a person as well. It will change how efficient and thorough you are in your work, and it will separate you from the pack. Your manager will recognize this. When your manager hands you a new assignment, there will be no annoying whining from you but a positive can-do response. As a manager, which would you prefer to have working for you? A person who complains and makes excuses, or a person who is willing to do what it takes to get the job done? I know I'd pick the person who accepts the job with a positive attitude.

20

Be Proactive

BE PROACTIVE! DO not be a passive worker waiting for someone to poke you with a stick or nudge you awake. I get frustrated by the workers I run across in meetings who, when asked about a follow-up, say, "I emailed them." Or "I left a message on their voicemail." Oh, that's brilliant! I guess timing is all up to whenever they get back to you, right?

Be proactive! An email or voicemail is a good first move, but follow up. Call again later in the day; send another email. Do they work at your site? Then go to their office. Ask a friend of theirs where they are. Hunt them down! Do you know how lame it sounds when you say, "I left them a voicemail/sent them an email"? It shows lack of initiative and ownership in the task for which you are responsible.

Proactivity on your part is a great way to demonstrate that you are in charge, you own the task, and you have it under control. As a project leader, I expect the project team to be on top of the task and doing what they can to get the work completed as soon as possible. You always want to evince the attitude of proactivity. Once you get a reputation for passive behavior, then you're a marked person. That isn't a good reputation to have in a dog-eat-dog world where little separates good from great.

Another way to demonstrate proactive behavior is to participate in meetings. You are in the meeting to contribute. Don't sit there and pretend to listen. Make sure you understand the discussion. Make sure you understand the implication of decisions. There may be a point in the project where you need to know that material so you make the right decision for your task. You should never leave a meeting without fully comprehending the topics covered. So be proactive, speak up, and learn!

I was in a meeting one time where we were reviewing a document and the word *Bis* kept coming up in the document. I had no idea what the word meant. But every time the word was mentioned, I saw the others nodding or saying nothing. I naturally assumed they knew what it meant. After a few times of this word coming up, I asked the project leader what it meant. Imagine my surprise when he said he didn't know nor did anyone else in the room! I guess I was the only one comfortable enough to admit I didn't know.

I said to the team, "We need to understand why this word is here and its purpose." After the meeting, I dug into the documentation but could find nothing related to the word. Some months later, I was vacationing in France when we came across a house with the number thirteen and next to the number that word *Bis*! I asked our guide what it meant. She replied that the house had been divided into two residences, but they needed to keep the same house number so they added the word *Bis*, which means in French "next to." Aha! I had our answer! When I got back, I explained the word's meaning to the team and added an explanation to the document for future reference. It does pay to ask when you don't know something.

Paying Attention in Meetings

Have you ever been in a meeting where the attendees have their laptops open and are typing or they are on their phones checking emails or texts? If so, why are they in the meeting? They obviously aren't listening, so how can they contribute? It makes the meeting facilitator's job more difficult in having to repeat his or her remarks or to reengage those not listening. In my opinion, it is rude to whoever is speaking.

This is especially frustrating in teleconferences. You are holding a teleconference, and you ask a question to the person on the phone. You don't get a response, so you ask the question again. Still no response, so you start asking for the person by calling their name. "John, John, are you there? Did you hear the question?" You even check the participant list to see if John is still there.

Suddenly he replies, "Sorry, I had you on mute. What was the question again?" I don't know what teleconference system you use, but with ours, when you're on mute, you hear the other speakers but they don't hear you. Typically what happens when someone is on mute, they often ask to have the question repeated. Obviously they weren't paying attention. This is a drawback to teleconference calls.

When people on the call are multitasking, it negatively impacts the quality of the meeting's dialogue. I suggest you set meeting ground rules. All laptops should be closed, and use of personal phones should be prohibited during the meeting.

21

Cultural Differences

IF YOU WORK at a company that has worldwide locations or deals with global companies, please be mindful of cultural differences. There's a funny story that illustrates potential problems you could face due to cultural differences.

Based on last year's turkey sales, a company places an order for one thousand turkeys from Japan. Honestly, I don't know why the company had to buy turkeys from Japan, but this is how the story goes, so work with me here. Well, it's a month before Thanksgiving, and the company notices that their advance orders are way, way down, and they may be stuck with a lot of extra inventory (i.e., unsold turkeys). So the company calls up the distributor in Japan they had placed the order with and tells them to cut the order in half. The distributor says, "Hai" (Japanese for "Yes"), and all is right with the world. The order is due two weeks prior to Thanksgiving, and the order arrives right on time. The company is quite pleased until they open the first shipping carton. The workers are aghast and frantically open all the shipping cartons. They call the owner out to the receiving dock, gesturing and pointing while explaining to the owner what they found. The owner is furious. Who's going to buy these turkeys? A potpie manufacturer maybe?

Why was he furious? He received his turkeys, all right, just as he stipulated. Every turkey was sliced right down the middle. Every turkey was cut in half. The owner got what he requested: his order was cut in half—literally.

Did the Japanese company do something wrong? From its point of view, no, they did exactly what was requested of them. They cut the order in half. Maybe if the company placing the order had stated the request in a different way, like, "Please change my order from one thousand to five hundred," the Japanese company would have gotten the order right.

This funny story points out that when dealing with other cultures, you must be very careful how you state your intentions. In Japan, the reply "Hai" (yes, remember?) does not necessarily mean they will do what you asked. In Japanese culture, replying "Hai" may mean they are simply acknowledging what you are saying; they do not necessarily understand what you are asking of them, so they may not do as you asked.

You need to be mindful of how you speak. English is translated literally, and the interpretation can end up being misleading. What would happen if you were looking at something that was really amazing, and you said, "Wow, that is sick"? Do you think that remark will be interpreted as you observing someone is ill, or will they know that it is slang for something that is cool? Be cautious about using slang. One thing you can do is to ask them to repeat your request so you can confirm what you said was understood.

Also, don't try to impress people from other countries

with your command of the English language. Which is better? Saying, "Scintillate, scintillate, asteroid diminutive" or "Twinkle, twinkle, little star"?

While in one of our overseas companies, we were working with the plant management and engineers on plans to make improvements in local product performance and supplier improvements. We had two plants in the country, and we invited a plant manager to meet us in the other plant to discuss how we could make the needed changes. The first day, all was proceeding as meetings like this typically play out. We arrived and spent the first half of the day getting the audiovisual equipment to work, making introductions, fixing the room temperature, allowing everyone to get food and drinks, and, of course, the obligatory management rah-rah speech reminding everyone how it was very important that "we" be successful.

Finally, with all that behind us, we could get to work. We reviewed what we wanted to accomplish, and the local team listened and nodded. We asked them questions about their processes and what we needed them to do. They kept nodding, and we thought things were going smoothly. The next day when we got together, a few of the plant participants were missing, being busy for some reason or another. As we went through the week, fewer and fewer of the local team showed up. We soon realized they weren't aligned with what we wanted to do, and they figured if they made themselves scarce, they wouldn't need to make the requested changes. By the end of the week, it was like *And Then There Were None*. They were not aligned, and instead of stating that to us, they just removed themselves from the discussion. We heard this through the grapevine. To rectify the situation, we had to get management to mandate their participation.

The Cultural Impact at Work

In Latin cultures, family is very important. It's polite to discuss how the workers' families are doing and inquire about their children. In German culture, this would be more appropriate after hours. Work comes first. Now, these are generalizations so don't get too upset. I do realize with the prevalence of the internet, people understand cultural differences more and more; but it's good to bear in mind a person's cultural bias.

One of the problems you will face with global companies is an out-of-sight, out-of-mind mentality: "You aren't here, so we don't need to listen to you," or "You'll leave in a few days, so we'll acknowledge what you want, but when you leave, we can go back to what we were doing." This isn't really a cultural difference, but more of an attitude issue. People don't like outsiders telling them what to do. I call it "xenophobic manu-facturing." A lot of the people at the plants I dealt with didn't like anyone who wasn't from their site telling them what to do. They would even go so far as to create local specifications and move requirements into these documents. Local documents were approved by local approvers, so no one outside the plant was required to approve such documents. This approach al-lowed the site to make changes without anyone away from the site knowing about them.

Another trick the plants would pull was to only convey what they thought you needed to know to get your approval. I ran into this a lot. The best way to counter this lack of clear communica-tion was to really know the product and processes so you could ask the right questions to get to the real reason for the change.

Above all, be respective of other cultures and their dif-ferences. Personally, I think it is great to get a chance to ex-perience other cultures.

22

Understanding Politics with Your Manager

KEEP YOUR BOSS in the loop, and as a boss, keep your direct reports in the loop. I had a role as an approver to ensure changes were properly documented and appropriate. There was a large project going on converting specifications into a new format. The department doing the conversion was supposed to be the only one converting the documents, but its workers would make product changes and try to sneak them through so they didn't have to go through our design change process, which would take more time. Typical behavior. They would seem to follow the rules, but when the rules impacted their needs, they bent them.

I found some discrepancies and rejected the changes to ensure they were corrected. What do you think the director did when he found out about my rejection? Did he call me? No. He went right to my manager and complained. What did my manager do? My manager negotiated a solution with the director. Then my manager told me about the conversation and the outcome and what I needed to do to allow the change to be approved.

Was this appropriate behavior by both the director and my manager? No, it was not. First, the director should have contacted me to discuss my reason for rejection and what options I would be agreeable with to allow the change to be approved. Second, when the director called my manager, my manager should have first asked the director if he had discussed the concern with me, and if he had not, then my manager should have told him to speak with me and call my manager *only* if he got to an impasse.

Unfortunately, in this scenario, both management positions behaved improperly. First, the director didn't work out the problem with me (was this a way to avoid direct conflict by leveraging authority to force the approval?), and second, my manager, by engaging with the director to get a resolution, undermined my authority. This approach took me out of the discussion. This made it a negotiation between the two of them, with me as the executor of their decision. They didn't follow the chain of responsibility.

As a manager, work through your direct reports. Do not allow other managers to circumvent your direct reports to get something done. This trivializes your direct reports and tells the managers that if they want something done, to talk to the manager and not the manager's direct reports.

I mentioned this to my manager, who—to his credit—immediately saw what his actions did. I asked if he had talked to the director and asked if he had spoken with me about the issue. My manager said he did not. I explained that he should only get involved if the director of the department and I could not reach a compromise; to get involved without allowing that conversation to take place meant that the director would always go right to him when there was a problem. This was also a subtle ploy by the director to undermine my credibility with my manager, so it was a form of aggressive power play. My manager promised to bear that in mind in the future. That didn't happen; the director is still circumventing me to this day.

To summarize, if you find yourself a manager one day, make sure you get involved in a situation only after the parties have exhausted all options with your direct reports. It's the only way to make sure your direct reports are respected. It's how they learn to handle difficult issues. It's also a way to indicate to management that they need to first work things through with your direct reports, and you are only to get involved when an impasse is reached.

23

Stones and Sand

EVER WONDER HOW some people seem to always effort-lessly get their work done? Then there are those who are always struggling and end up late, causing delays as the team tries to get additional resources to get the work done. These two types of people represent opposites in their approach to work. The person who's always late may be a procrastinator, or just bad at structuring the day and work schedule. On the other hand, there are people who seem to get their work done effortlessly. What's their secret? One reason may be that these people have a lot of experience and have been at the job a long time, so experience allows them to make quick decisions. Another reason may be that these conscientious individuals have figured time management out and simply have good work ethics.

Earlier, you read about eating the elephant one bite at a time. Well, there's another aspect you may not be aware of: being good at optimizing your time. What I found that works for me and helped me get my projects done on time or ahead of schedule was following the elephant example, but also moving from one project to another throughout the day. This helped me move all my projects forward and kept me current on my project status in case I was asked about it. I found it helped stimulate my thinking as well. Taking a mental break by shifting your focus helps improve your ability to think. This is because you're using your brain in a different manner, each project having different demands in concentration and analytics. This way of working helps refresh your brain and your mental approach to the tasks.

I suggest you work on a problem, and when you feel like you're losing focus, stop and work on something else. Later, go back to the original project with a refreshed attitude; often, this has led me to a viable solution. What does this have to do with the title of this chapter? Well, picture your projects as stones, and your manager's last-minute requests as sand. You always have filler time; it's just a matter of time management and discipline. I've found that I always carried an enormous workload and was always busy. I liked that because the day flew by and I always felt a sense of accomplishment at the end of the day. Maybe I'm old-fashioned in that respect, but I liked that at the end of the day, I felt like I had accomplished something.

By always cycling through my projects several times in the course of a day, I consistently find some time to add in another task. This is the sand. If my manager needed to get something done, I would offer to help. After all, I'm there to support my manager. Now if it was something I dreaded, I wouldn't volunteer, but the point is that you always have slack time. You just need to recognize how you're spending your time and challenge yourself with the question "Am I working efficiently and effectively?" If you can get yourself into this mode of operating, you will find that tasks are not as daunting as they first appear, and you really can accomplish a lot with not much more effort.

Don't get me wrong. There were days when I got overwhelmed and I couldn't figure out what to do next. At times, I would have tons of emails still unopened, voicemails unanswered, and the weight of my unfinished projects on my shoulders. In this instance, I stopped everything, picked one thing to focus on, and made the decision to stay with that task until it was done. In this case, I prioritized completion of a report by closing my email program and taking the phone off the hook. By the end of the day, I had the report completed. I felt like I had a small victory, and that was one thing off my plate. From that point on, I felt less stressed, and my mental logjam had disappeared. Try it. I'm pretty sure you will find it helps cope with your workload. For some people, it's just not in their DNA to function this way. If that's the case, then you need to ask yourself, "Am I in the right job?"

24

What You See Is What You Get

YOU HAVE THAT new job, and you really want to impress the boss and start making a name for yourself, right? Well, one thing that's often overlooked is what you write and, more importantly, how you write.

For example, we all know that first impressions count a lot. If someone were to come to an interview in an expensive suit, but it was ill-fitting and wrinkled, you might be hesitant to hire them. Would you dine in a restaurant that was dirty? Would you shop at a store that was unorganized, wares lying haphazardly around the store? Appearances do matter. We do judge books by their covers. Don't kid yourself; we all have unconscious bias.

This all relates again to implied perceptions. Your emails and reports are your everyday résumés. They reflect you and your work ethic. Have you ever received an email in all caps? Ever get a report where you cannot follow the flow of thought? You think to yourself, *If this is how they write a report, I wonder if the data and analysis are really correct.*

I've found that problem in a lot of situations. It's almost more important how you present the information than the information itself. I have tried this. I sent out draft reports with some nonsense sentences as an experiment, but because they looked professional, no one questioned them. Unbelievable? Yes, but true.

There are several issues you need to keep in mind when writing a report.

First, who is your audience? Knowing the audience your document is addressing is essential. Bear in mind as a secondary consideration who else may see it. Write at a level that's appropriate to the audience and the secondary audience that may see it (e.g., management). One thing that's often overlooked is what you did and why. Too many times, I've seen a completion report for a project written with key information missing.

Another issue is what I consider the most important part of any completed task: Can someone repeat the work from what you wrote? Are they able to replicate the testing and so on? I always review my reports to see if I have included all the details. How did I do the work, what was done, and why? Why did I make the conclusions I did? What was important to the testing and why? Basically, think five years down the road. Could someone five years from now read the report and replicate everything you did? If so, then you wrote a comprehensive report. You cannot assume others know what you know. I also try to write at a high school level to explain what I did so anyone can follow. Please don't try to impress people with your polysyllabic words and BS. You impress people better when they can understand what you did. People can detect a dissembler despite what you may think.

One way to look at your writing is to ask yourself if someone could understand how you got from A to C. I have read too many reports where the author assumes you know what they did and why. Documentation is critical. Document why you did what you did and why you made the decisions you did, why the results are correct or not, and so on. Basically, you need to have a clear paper trail. Look at it from the perspective of an auditor. What questions would an auditor ask, and have you included the information to answer the questions completely and comprehensively?

25

To Do It Once, Do It Right

I ONCE DEVELOPED a new way to create one of our component specifications along with a central database format. I left the department before it was fully implemented, and the department finished up the implementation. This involved revising and standardizing the dimensions. However, I wanted to standardize the names of the components and their identification format, as we were currently working with five different formats. I also wanted only headquarters to create or modify the component specifications. The reason is that over time, with multiple sites changing specifications, there were so many errors and discrepancies that the best way to minimize errors and create consistency was to make one group responsible for the specifications. The underlying rationale for this approach was that the other sites were manufacturing sites and that's all they should focus on—manufacturing. They also weren't the designated design house. Creating new components or specifications wasn't their responsibility; that was research and development's job.

Research and development (R&D) saw it differently. R&D just wanted to get the database done, so they uploaded files with few of the needed corrections and submitted the changes. Did R&D update the identification formats, fix the descriptions, or align dimensions between the same components? No. R&D explained that there simply wasn't time or resources. It was more important that they transfer the files. Besides, those changes could be done later when they would have time and resources. The thing was that if R&D professed that they didn't have the time now to fix things, what was the chance of them having the time and resources later? If R&D did it later, they would need to repeat all the approval documentation as well—was that really more efficient? I asked R&D, "If you don't have the time now, how do you know you'll have the time later?"

Did this approach really standardize things? No, it was handled this way just to get the database up and running. R&D never really went back to fix all the disconnects and discrepancies.

So what was really accomplished? We got a single database, but most of the problems we had were still there. R&D continued to allow other sites to make changes that often weren't caught or checked.

And how did this all turn out? Well, the manager moved on to another role, and the follow-ups? So far, they *still* aren't done.

Taking the extra time while you have the resources you need is the correct way to fix a problem. You never know if you'll have the time later, so why put off what you can do now when you have the attention of management to get the problems rectified?

I never understand this lazy approach to fixing things. It's like putting off patching a roof. Sooner or later, you will need to fix the roof, and in the meantime, your wallboard and insulation are going to be damaged; thus, the cost of a new roof will be increased by the additional repairs.

That's why I always went by the maxim of "To do it once, do it right." Another way I would put it is "Work hard to be lazy." In other words, I would put in the extra effort to ensure things were right so I didn't have to redo something or go back to fix something. That attitude is the lazy part. Why get stuck on fixing something that you did already? I want to move on to other things like new ideas.

Would you like a contractor to "kind of" repair a problem and come back again and charge you for additional work? I viewed this approach by research and development as lazy and, more importantly, it wasn't taking responsibility nor being accountable. Sadly, management, having no idea of what the benefit was and without understanding the implications, didn't step in and require them to do it right.

Let me give you another perspective on "To do it once, do it right." We were having new and complicated robotic test equipment designed and built. Unfortunately, the idea of automating the test was much more complicated than we first thought. We had to struggle through root cause investigations, one after another. Meanwhile, our deadline was fast approaching. One faction wanted us to ship the machine with the known issues and then fix them in-house. This way, we would meet the deadline for delivery.

I was not of this faction. I felt that we needed to fix the machine before shipping it. That the best way to accomplish this was to have it at the design house, where the mechanics would work on it and resolve the issues. If we shipped it, then we would have to negotiate costs to send their engineers to our plant. This expense wasn't in the project budget, and we would have no leverage to ensure they would come to our site. Keeping the machine in their building canceled any excuse their engineers might have not to work on the machine if it was shipped. Yes, this would delay the shipping, but I felt that it was better to be late and right than to be on time and wrong. No one would remember that the machine was late if it worked correctly, but if it was on time and didn't work, well then, that would be remembered.

I won out in the end, and the machine was shipped late, but it was operational. No one remembered it was late; management was happy to see the new technology successfully working.

26

Risk

EARLY IN YOUR career, take risks—they should be calculated, but take them! You have nothing to lose. In the beginning of your career, you're still trying to define who you are and what you want to do. As you grow in your career, you acquire responsibilities. You get married, you buy a home, you have children. All of these add to your responsibilities, your obligations, and it makes it difficult for you to be willing to take a chance.

However, when you're starting out, what do you have to lose? You're not married, you don't have a house—most likely you're renting—and you have no children. You can easily recover from any setback because you have less to recover from. That's why I suggest trying as many things as possible early in your career.

I told my kids growing up to try different things. Until you try something, you don't know what you like and don't like. You need to challenge yourself to try things that may not be readily appealing or look like they're a good fit to your persona. This is the only way you can begin to define who you are.

As you grow older, your tastes change and your interests evolve. By having tried different experiences early in your career, you're in a better position to identify what you may not have liked. But now, with the benefit of time and experience, you might find yourself gravitating to these new ventures that you once shied away from.

Your life will be so much more fulfilling when you take risks early in your career. The added benefit is that you also will gain broader experiences to draw from when solving problems and dealing with people from different careers. Having been there, you'll have a better understanding of how different people think and how different roles provide different perspectives.

New experiences will help you identify your strengths and weaknesses. Trying out different ideas early on helps you get a better sense of where your passion lies. This then helps you focus on developing your career in the areas of your passion. You may start out working in an area and enjoy the work, but if you didn't try anything else, how do you know that's the path of your true passion? The more you challenge yourself, the more you push yourself to find out your limits. These challenges will help shape your career. You'll reap the benefits down the road later.

Quite honestly, I took whatever job was the most appealing at the time because back then it wasn't hard to find a decent-paying job. Each of my jobs taught me something. I learned a bit more of what I liked to do, what part of the job I enjoyed, and what part I didn't like. I also learned the skills associated with that job so I could apply them to my next line of work. You never know—that job you decided to take as a "holdover until something better comes along" may turn out to be the best career choice you make.

Never ignore an opportunity. Do not be afraid. Trust in yourself, believe in yourself, and challenge yourself. The rewards will be priceless.

27

Pay Attention to the Little Things

DID YOU EVER take a walk in the woods, just walking with no real destination in mind, enjoying the peacefulness, the quiet, the beauty? You walk along, meandering among the trees, ducking under low branches while gazing up at the canopy of limbs overhead, marveling at the size of the trees. Suddenly, you fall flat on your face. "Ouch! What just happened? Oh, that hurts!" You sit up and check for broken bones and cuts. Okay, all seems to be good and working right. "What caused me to fall?" You look around and see a small root protruding up ever so slightly from the forest floor. Apparently, your toe caught on the root and tripped you.

As you were walking, you moved around trees and maneuvered around branches, stepped over fallen logs, but it was the small root that you overlooked or dismissed as something unimportant. This happens while working on projects. We see the big things, the obvious things to be concerned with, but we often dismiss the little things, the small things, and those that don't quite fit into our plans. We dismiss them as unimportant or trivial, only to have them rear up at the most inopportune time to trip up our project timing.

If something doesn't quite fit, take the extra time to understand it. I've been involved in projects where someone asked a question, and the team member responsible replied that it wasn't important. Maybe it was. Take the time to check, to verify, and go with your gut feeling. You may avoid a setback with just a few minutes of extra digging.

However, there's a fine line between getting too caught up in the minutiae and keeping to the big picture. That's a different problem altogether. We can get so caught up in details (the trees) that we fail to see the big picture (the forest) and miss the relationship between them. This takes some practice and experience. Another way of looking is to visualize something from one thousand feet and ten thousand feet. Just like flying, at one thousand feet, you see all kinds of details, but at ten thousand feet, you lose those details and instead see a larger picture and how everything is connected as a whole. There are pros and cons to both views, and you can learn a lot if you can get yourself to look at a detail and then see how it fits into the big picture.

It's kind of like when you're assembling a jigsaw puzzle. You hold a piece of the puzzle in your hand and study its shape to see where it may fit, but you also look at the puzzle as you have completed it so far (or cheat and look at the box cover) to see where the piece would likely fit. Sometimes you don't have enough information to know where the piece goes, so you put it aside. Later, when other pieces are placed, you recall this piece and now have enough information to place the piece in the puzzle. This is the same as filing away a concern until you have more information.

Always pay attention to the little things, see how they fit into the larger picture, and do not dismiss something just because it seems trivial if you don't have enough information to make an informed decision about it.

28

Mistakes Happen, But They Can Be Life Lessons

LOOK, IT'S INEVITABLE; we all make mistakes. I like to refer to them as *experience*. I would say to my manager, "If you don't want me to make mistakes, then I will do nothing." Seems a bit haughty, but there's a strong underlying element of truth to the statement.

I have to assume a person is trying to do the best job possible and is putting forth the best effort. You can only make your decisions based on data, experience, intuition, expert input, and experimentation. Despite all of these avenues of input, you can still make mistakes. You can overlook data, misinterpret data, or just plain lack input that's needed, though no one was aware of that. You see, mistakes provide insight into the unknown, into obscure interactions or inputs. Armed with the root cause of the mistake, you can make intelligent changes that result in improved product or quality.

I have sometimes learned more from my mistakes than from getting things right by dumb luck. It's often said that experience is another way to say *mistake*. This is why those "old associates" you see at work seem to know all the answers. They're probably providing answers that are based on what they learned from mistakes, their trials and errors, their screwups, and just plain carelessness. So don't be afraid to fail. In the long run, mistakes are golden gems of knowledge.

29

Write Right

IF YOU NEED to write procedures, specifications, or any type of documentation, there are a few things to keep in mind. The first thing to remember is that not everyone has the same level of understanding. You may believe what you're writing is easily understood, but how do you know all readers or users of the document have the same training or expertise as yourself?

To accommodate this, I always suggest writing as if you're explaining something to your parents. For example, which of the following is easier to understand? "Bifurcate the cylinder longitudinally," or "Split the rod lengthwise"? Mistakes can easily occur if your writing is too complicated, especially if what you write requires translation. Keep your words simple.

The second thing to bear in mind is to ensure all necessary information is included. The benefit of this approach is that it forces you to capture all necessary details so someone can replicate what you did.

I had a document to review where a step in the test method

read like this: "Mix ingredients and heat until hot." So how do I know the ingredients are mixed, and how hot is hot? Here's how I had them rewrite the line: "Mix the two ingredients until completely dissolved. This occurs when the solution becomes clear. Heat the solution to a minimum 100 degrees Celsius for a minimum of 10 minutes, no more than 15 minutes." All the additional information ensures the solution is mixed the same way each time; nothing important is assumed.

In reporting on testing, be sure to write so you can accurately repeat the testing. Imagine you need to repeat the testing two years from now. Could you accurately repeat all the steps of the testing, how the data was analyzed, and the logic of your decisions from what you wrote? Someone else may need to replicate your work later, which could be impossible if you're not detailed enough in documenting what you did and why.

I refer to this as explaining how you got from A to C. A document should be clear in how you progressed from start (A) to finish (C). What steps you took and why, what decisions you made and why, the data conclusions and the why of the conclusions. If you adhere to these points, your documents will be clear, concise, and informative to anyone reading them. If the document is ever subjected to an audit, the auditor should have no problem following your logic and coming to the same conclusion. Thoroughly written and comprehensive documents provide a clear path and understanding to an auditor. This avoids the auditor asking questions or raising challenges that you may not be able to answer.

Your Coworkers

30

Worrying about Others

I'M SURE YOU'VE encountered those coworkers who seem to spend their entire day going from one cubicle to another. They talk about what other people are doing, then talk about how busy they are. What do you want to say to them when they keep on coming into your cubicle? "You must not be working that hard if you have time to worry about what other people are doing."

Or if they are worrying about what others are doing or "getting away with," do you want to say to them, "You don't know what issues they're having, or what their manager told them to do. Maybe they're working after work or on weekends." I suggest to "cube-hoppers" to focus on what they must do rather than what others are doing or not doing. You don't know what issues others are dealing with.

I really think there are several factors going on with cube-hoppers. One, they are trying to fish for gossip or get your viewpoint so they can start something. Or two, the cube-hoppers are just trying to avoid working. Very simply, they are afraid to start on something because they are not sure what to do, so they'd rather talk about it to others. Another reason for their behavior may be that cube-hoppers are trying to figure out how you would handle their work by asking you questions. Maybe they are just trying in a roundabout way to get insight on how you would handle something because they don't know what to do themselves and don't want anyone to know they are confused or at a loss and are subtly trying to find options. Whatever the reason, cube-hoppers are disruptive and generally are not working very hard.

Hopefully, there aren't too many cube-hoppers at your workplace.

31

Attitude and Aptitude

I HAVE INTERVIEWED a lot of people, and I have found that some people are good interviewers. Some should abstain from doing so, mainly because (a) they do not know what they want in a candidate, or (b) they just do not know how to probe and ask questions to get the answers they are looking for.

If you find yourself a manager and in a position to hire, consider the following.

I have always sworn that in interviews, attitude is as important as aptitude. It does no good to have people who are book smart and knowledgeable if they can't

- communicate,
- work with others,
- work hard,
- accept responsibility, and
- socialize with coworkers and customers.

Any of these, or a combination of any of these, would more than neutralize the benefit of intelligence.

I would love to have people who are intelligent work for me, but if they don't take their job seriously, then how can you optimize their talents? Don't you think you would have to devote more work in managing them? Those who can be self-sufficient would generate the work you expect with minimal supervision. That's the type of person you want to hire. You need to explore and weigh attitude as much as brainpower. Would you prefer to have someone work for you where you

- have to constantly explain everything and correct their work; or
- can give basic instructions to them, and from there they would know enough to execute your instructions without further assistance?

Look for the go-getters, those whose résumés impress you as people with a plan, a focus, a career objective. Pay as much attention to *how* someone answers your questions as what they say. Your decision will make your job as a manager either easier or more difficult. Attitude trumps aptitude almost every time. A person with drive and ambition will learn in the process. A person who lacks attitude lacks motivation and passion. The type of worker you want in your department or on your team will become obvious by the comparison.

32

Project Teams and Project Leaders

Project Team Members

You may find yourself on a project team where it seems some people just will not do their work or be on time with deliverables or not evince a sense of urgency. You ask yourself why these people act this way. There are varied reasons for this. Take new hires, for example. They don't have the network or knowledge of the product or processes to draw from. They're given a task with responsibility and asked to get it done. Since they're new, they may be worried that if they don't look good, they'll get fired or viewed as incompetent. What do they do in response? They take an enormous amount of time to ensure their work is correct before they deliver it. This delays the deliverables, but from their perspective, they're protecting themselves, a form of CYA (cover your ass).

Another behavior characteristic of some team members

when they do not have an assignment done is to explain the task as belonging to someone else or some other department. Or then there is "victim think," which translates to, "I was sick," or "I had another priority," or "My manager asked me to work on something else, so I had to put this on hold." It's important to realize that everyone has a personal reason for certain behaviors and actions. Lack of confidence is just one.

Another factor may be the employee is unsure about what to do and maybe has no one to go to for guidance. He or she may be afraid to ask or tell the project leader for fear of reprisals or that the project leader will go to their manager and complain. Team members may also have conflicting priorities. The team member's department may be "supporting" your project, but the department has its own priorities that are quietly taking precedence over your project.

There are many reasons why a team doesn't function smoothly and deliverables are not completed on time. Try to understand what may motivate a person's behavior. Basically, everyone wants to do a good job, but often it's self-confidence or lack of understanding that can interfere. Yes, there are others who just don't work. They're the ones who manage to dodge responsibility by using their political connections or by playing word games with emails and conversations. You will not change these people, so avoid them and get them off the team as soon as you can—you'll be better for it.

Project Leaders

As a project leader, find the strengths and weaknesses of your team members and utilize them to optimize the members' strengths. You should coach and support from the sidelines so, in the end, the team members feel like they did it themselves, while all along you were behind the scenes helping through your network. "Hi, Janet, I have Bill coming to you with a part approval. Appreciate if you can review and approve it. I already reviewed it, and it looks okay to me." Then when Bill comes, Janet is prepared, knows the purpose of the document, and knows you, so she will have a greater tendency to accommodate your needs than if it were just Bill, whom she doesn't know. In that case, Janet would take more time to review and consider the approval.

One major thing to remember when running a project: team members will inevitably raise issues only at meetings. How often did you hear people in a meeting say they have an issue or a problem, yet they never said anything until the meeting? Get your team members to tell you *before* a meeting. They should inform you as the project leader when the problem occurs so you don't lose the time in between to work on the problem.

Meetings should be no more than a heads-up on where things are and what's expected next week. They're not for airing issues—that's what the communication between the project leader and the team members is for. Treat each team member as a contractor picked for expertise. Your role as project leader is to coordinate the contractors. When a problem hits the project, make sure no one waits until the problem is fixed. Ensure the team that everything is okay and tell them to keep moving forward while you and the impacted team member(s) work on the issue.

Too often when a problem hits a team, everyone stops working, and you lose precious time. The natural tendency of team members is to look at the problem as a reprieve from the project schedule. Now they have time freed up to work on other commitments. If a problem does occur, you need to address it immediately before it gets out of hand and people start saying, "Project _____ is in trouble. Did you hear ..." That's to be avoided at all costs. It gives the project a bad image and delays work, and as I mentioned, anyone supporting the project peripherally will think his or her support is not as urgent. They will move their work for you to the bottom of the pile. Their perception is you're not in a hurry and their deliverable can wait. This is the last thing you want them thinking!

As a project leader, your job is managing egos and project communications and working behind the scenes to help facilitate your team members in their tasks. The more effort you put into this, the better your chances of success. Your job as project leader is to mold your team into a cohesive, highly functioning group. Guide your team through the stages of team building:

- forming (getting your team together)
- storming (working through the team dynamics of personalities and conflicts)
- norming (team coming together to work as one)
- performing (seemingly effortless execution)

At times, this may take some effort. I led a project once where I was given a packaging engineer whom everyone said was always late, his work always contained errors, and he never seemed to understand what was needed. At the end of my project, the packaging engineer had his work done ahead of schedule with no errors. The packaging engineer came to me and said he would work with me again on any project and was happy to have been a part of the team. What did I do to evince this kind of behavior and attitude from the packaging engineer? I talked to him constantly. "What are your issues?

What do you see will be your main obstacles?" I would work on his obstacles or what he perceived as obstacles when he wasn't confident he could resolve them. Thus, when the packaging engineer came to the point in his job that he expected the obstacle, it wasn't there. Very simple, yet a profound impact. I did this with all my team members. At my request, all my team members had to tell me when they could deliver and what they would need to meet their date.

Good teamwork is all about effort and negotiation. The team felt ownership and didn't feel rushed or harried. It was because they always knew what was expected of them and when. This is the way to truly manage a project and project team members.

You're in the trees, but can you see the forest? Sometimes we're so caught up in the details we fail to understand how they fit into the larger picture. Are the details relevant? Are they necessary to the overall project? Moreover, are they *your* responsibility?

I have often seen team members try to do everything or want to do everything connected with their task. It's the way they ensure their task is done properly; at least in their mind, that's the way they think.

This ties into roles and responsibilities. A good project leader will recognize when team members aren't delivering because they aren't focusing on their immediate tasks. A good project leader will be aware of what each team member is doing so he or she can adjust the focus of the team member. I was on a project where the project leader wouldn't make a decision. Well, I need to take that back. He did make decisions on when and where he would travel for the project, but in a meeting, he never made a decision. In fact, in one teleconference, he had a manufacturing site start to draft a document, which was my role along with the project's quality engineer. When I pointed out to him that he shouldn't have two groups working on the same thing and he needed to maintain clear roles and responsibilities, he replied that was not his job.

The main function of a project leader is to define team member roles and responsibilities and make decisions with team input so the project moves forward smoothly and maintains target dates.

The second role of a project leader is to remove obstacles in the team's way. Then teams can focus on delivering, and the project leader is one step ahead clearing the way, ensuring matériel, resources, and so on are available when needed. This is how a smoothly running team should work.

Team Meetings Tips

First, team meetings should be short and should *only* give the project team an overall update and any broad project updates with upcoming target dates and milestones. "Aren't team meetings to get the team together to work through problems and project issues?" you might ask. Put simply, they are not for that purpose.

You *do* need the team to solve project problems, but do you need the *whole* team? Do you need the planning person, the finance person, or the packaging engineer to solve a technical problem with, say, an electrical component? Is that an effective use of a team member's time? No, it's not. Are there other consequences of using the team meeting to solve problems? Yes, there are.

If you're using team meetings to solve project issues, what do you think the team members are going to do? They'll wait until the scheduled team meeting to bring their project problems to your attention. So what happens to the other four workdays? Think the team members are working on the project? Not really, or not as much as they could, since they're waiting for the team meeting to work on their problem—the problem the team will solve in an hour, just like on TV.

You know that's not going to happen. So you set up another working meeting with those you need and a few others who want to attend to see what the decision will be. Some may use the meeting as an excuse for not working on their other responsibilities. Or the team members know there's this "big" problem that will "hold up the project," so they can back off and not work as hard. Then small delays start to creep into the project from one team member or another, slowly accumulating into one *big* project delay. I liken it to having an arsonist light fires while you're trying to put them out. You don't realize there's an arsonist making your life miserable. Now how about that timeline? Looking good still? Deadline looks like it's staring you in the face?

Another drawback is that team members, knowing there's a problem, will naturally concentrate on other responsibilities because they know that "it will be a while before they fix *that* problem." So that timeline slips a little more ... and a little more ...

I don't recommend using project team meetings to solve project problems. As a project leader, I encouraged my project team members to let me know immediately when they ran into an issue. Then I worked with them to arrange what was needed to get the issue solved. That was one of my roles as a project leader—to eliminate obstacles for my team members. Meanwhile, I didn't have the other team members involved— only the team members who were relevant to the problem—so they could continue to focus on what they needed to do for the project. Then, at the team meetings, I informed the other team members of what was going on, along with any adjustments to the project schedule. I kept a calm demeanor so team members felt that everything was under control. This way, we moved on and stayed on target, or as close as possible.

Now that you have this resolved, let's turn to the team members themselves. Team function relies heavily on the attitude and competence of the individuals on the team. This is a good reason why it is important to get good team members assigned to your project.

Let me give you an example of how this worked for me. I was given the job of project leader for a new medical device. The packaging engineer assigned to my project had a reputation for delivering late, with the packaging full of mistakes. He was a nervous type who would get things messed up easily and was quickly flustered. I immediately knew I would have my hands full.

So at the beginning of the project, I sat down with the packaging engineer. I asked him what information was necessary for the package design. Essentially, I was learning the basic needs to design a package and what other team members would have to provide as inputs to the design. Another aspect I inquired of him was about the typical issues he ran into in past projects. He was very candid and remarked that he never had a project leader ask him these things before. He detailed to me where he typically ran into issues and why. With this information, I went ahead and planned with the other team members to ensure he had what he needed when he needed it. Is this something he could have done? Of course, but as project leader, would it have been in my best interest to wait while he tried to figure out what he *wasn't* able to do in past projects? No, the best way was to get him what he needed, not to distract him and then explain what I did, how I did it, and why I did it. I was teaching him on the fly.

The approach worked well. He had his packaging done *ahead* of time, and there were no problems with the packaging. After the project, he thanked me and told me he would be happy to work again with me on a project. He also thanked me for teaching him things that would help him in the future. I thanked him as well, as he was dutiful and was a solid team member throughout the project. He had a new level of confidence and was a much-improved packaging engineer after that.

Projects are like building a house. Each team member is a contractor with a specialty—plumber, heating technician, carpenter, painter, mason. In building a house, do you sit down with the plumber to work out a painting problem? Do you want the carpenter to figure out what size ducts to run for the air-conditioning? No, of course not, so why do you do that with projects? If I had a problem building the house where I couldn't figure out where to run a duct, I could get the heating technician and the carpenter together to work out the options but let the siding contractor continue to put up siding. They're not involved or affected.

When people are asked what makes a team successful, they often reply communication. I disagree. Yes, communication is critical, but what makes communication happen? Trust. Trust is the key to any successful team. The team members trust each other, support each other, and speak to each other outside of team meetings. When you have trust, you have relationships that are supportive and conscientious. Trust fosters communication. It is often spontaneous among team members on subjects that are unrelated to the project. This happens because team members want to spend time with each other.

As a project leader, if you can establish trust among your team, you have found the key to team success. Trust fosters communication, and communication fosters support, timely problem-solving, and efficient timelines. Team members genuinely enjoy being with each other and work outside of their area of expertise and responsibility to support one another. This is when a team is truly running at peak output—often greater than the sum of the parts.

So what do you as a project leader need to develop in your team? Trust.

I hope this may provide you with some things to think about when you start your next project as either a team member or a project leader.

33

Darn, I Did Not See That Coming!

HAVE YOU EVER been in a meeting, and someone drops a bombshell on you? You walk into the meeting thinking everything is okay, and then someone announces that process A isn't working because of something you did. Or you go into a meeting thinking everyone is aligned to a strategy, only to have one or two state a completely different grand design. The team goes into a spiral of disarray, and you fight a seemingly losing battle trying to get the team back together.

Situations like this happen frequently. Sometimes they're due to politics or personal agendas. Sometimes things fall apart just because someone doesn't like another person, and he or she just doesn't want to go along with an idea. This is a less-than-ideal situation and can go south quickly if it's played out in front of a customer or supplier, let alone in front of your manager, when you had reassured him that everything was copacetic.

Never, never disagree in front of a customer or a supplier, or basically before anyone not employed by your company. That's akin to airing dirty laundry in front of your neighbors. If you're blindsided by a completely different opinion in a meeting with a customer or supplier, I suggest you calm down, try to put on a poker face, and say to the offending individual, "You raise an interesting point that we should look into further. Would you mind if we table that for now and go through the rest of the agenda? We can circle back to it if we have time, but I think I would prefer that we discuss it with the rest of the team. Is that okay with everyone?" There are other ways to defuse the situation, but the idea isn't to escalate the issue into a confrontation and appear dysfunctional to the customer or supplier; you want to present a unified front at all times.

Disagreements or changes of mind are a potential reality. Sometimes they occur because additional information is revealed. There's nothing wrong with changing your mind or your position on a subject, but you shouldn't do that in front of customers or suppliers.

If you're visiting a customer or supplier, be sure to discuss all topics you think may come up and decide beforehand who will field the question. I suggest even having a phrase or statement you all agree to as a warning signal to the team. Something like, "That's an interesting point that we should take back to our XXX department to get their input." Something that denotes a follow-up but is vague and not specific. Your team will know immediately that the subject is now taboo and to move on to something else. This approach deflects, defers, and delays until you can make an agreed-upon decision. Of course, you need to make a commitment to the other side on when you will respond to the issue, but only state a general time frame such as four weeks, two weeks, or by the end of the month. After all, you told them you needed time to review the issue, so they will understand that's something that will take time. Now if they want an immediate response, then negotiate a response deadline.

There are two points I'm trying to convey here. One, do not blindside your manager or anyone in authority over you. Two, do not argue or objectively disagree in front of customers or suppliers—do that behind closed doors. If it's a subject that requires an immediate response, ask the customer or supplier if you can retire to a conference room with your team to discuss it. I would be surprised if that request were denied.

If you're in a meeting of this nature and your manager comes out of left field with a proposal and blindsides you— well, deal with it. Stop talking and let it go. Your manager may be privy to additional information, or your manager is making the decision by him or herself. Just let it ride. Later, in private, you can ask your manager why he or she said whatever, but don't challenge or question your manager in front of customers or suppliers. What do you do if what your manager says is completely and utterly wrong? And what if the customer or supplier agrees, and the decision is finalized? We do work under incompetent managers every now and then.

You can professionally and discreetly request a word with your manager in private at the earliest chance you have to politely interrupt. Maybe saying something like, "Ms./Mr. Hewitt, before we discuss this further, can I meet with you now for a minute? I need some points clarified. I hope you don't mind."

That may not be diplomatic, and perhaps you can think of a better, subtler way to frame things, but the point is you need to stop this situation now before it goes too far. If it's indeed the wrong decision, what do you think your manager will say to you later? Maybe something like, "Wilson, why didn't you speak up at the meeting and tell me that?" Suddenly, your manager's bad decision is all your fault. Bummer, but shore up your energy and temporarily accept the blame.

Before an important meeting, regardless of the situation, never assume alignment and verify even a few hours prior. You never know if last-minute information will surface that might end up changing the picture or the direction. Also, it's not a bad idea to work out a coded phrase with your manager beforehand. It does come back to expectations, doesn't it? Expectations of you and of your manager. But conflicting expectations is what you're always trying to avoid, both in business and with your career. Planning for the worst but expecting the best is never a bad thing.

Another perspective to consider at work is WIIFT (what's in it for them?). Sometimes we're put off by how someone reacts to something we said, or we're taken aback by how an employee completes a task—taking too long, being less than thorough, or just being incomplete. We are quick to dismiss them as incompetent or lazy. Sometimes we need to be a bit more empathetic. What's in it for them? What's their motivation? Sometimes I have seen poor work by someone, but it's not due to inabilities; it can be a result of overwork or personal stress. Don't be so quick to judge. Try to find out if there's an underlying issue before condemning someone.

The same is true when you need something from someone and it's taking forever to get it. Sometimes a task isn't done promptly because it's not in the person's best interest. His or her manager may require support for your project to be put on hold because their department had another priority.

Don't be quick to conclude a missed deadline is because a person doesn't care. Of course, it's that person's responsibility to control expectations (see how this works?) and inform you where he or she is with timing. Some people just don't see that as their responsibility. That said, if the task is important to you, then why have you not contacted the person to get an update or see what you can do to help them? Before you jump down someone's throat, ask yourself, "What is in it for them? What is their motivation?" A little empathy can go a long way.

Your Company

34

Warning! Nonstick Project Leader Ahead!

YOU'VE JUST BEEN put on a project with a known nonstick project leader. You poor team member! Get out! Get out now!

There's nothing worse than a nonstick project leader—not to be confused with a snake oil salesman.

These project leaders *never* take responsibility and are masters at turning the tables and finding scapegoats. It will never be them, they will never document a decision they make, and they will never allow themselves to be put into a position where they must make the decision.

I supported a project with one, and it was painful. I was the project's problem; I was the reason the project was delayed; I was the reason for missed deadlines. I was consulting as a design quality engineer due to my product and process experience, having done a similar project earlier. In that case, the project was going on for two years. They asked me to get involved. I resolved the issues and worked out a validation plan, and we completed the project successfully.

Working with this project leader, you wouldn't know that. Have you ever heard statements like these? If so, you're dealing with a nonstick project leader.

- "I know nothing about validation, but I don't understand why we need to do this."
- "Now I'm not an expert on design control—all of you are—but I don't understand why we need to follow design control."
- "Someone needs to tell me why we have to follow design control. Who should that be?"

I was responsible for developing an overall master validation strategy, but the project leader spoke to the site where we were going to do a transfer and asked them to start drafting the master validation strategy. Apparently, he told them in a one-on-one meeting to create the strategy. During a team meeting, I asked what they were doing, and he said, "A master validation strategy."

"That's my responsibility," I said.

Being a nonstick project leader, he replied, "I sent the minutes, and it was discussed in meetings. What's your problem?"

"You are the project leader," I replied, "and responsible for the roles and responsibilities of the team members."

"I am *not* responsible for roles and responsibilities."

Nonstick project leaders are to be avoided at all costs. Get yourself off any project they run. They will play the blame game with perfection. You will not beat them at their own game, so do not try. The worst part is management doesn't see this at all. They think the project leader is doing a wonderful job and should get a bonus for successfully and professionally dealing with all the issues. This is a good example of why management needs to be aware of what's going on and how things are getting done.

35

The Snowball Effect

HAVE YOU EVER experienced working on a simple change, and it suddenly goes spiraling out of control, becoming more and more complicated as you try to work on it? Sometimes the simplest solution can turn out to be the more complicated solution due to the systems it must work within.

We were introducing a new product code to accommodate testing required by the government. The samples were to be tested at an outside facility. To ensure the samples weren't compromised prior to testing, they were shipped at a controlled temperature. This was accomplished by using a purchased kit consisting of insulation panels and cold packs.

The final manufacturing site would have to order these kits, but they balked at doing this. Their management's position was that they might not remember to order the kits. We suggested they order stock, and when the stock got low, order more. Simple, right? They were ordering cardboard stock and consumables for other shipping, so why couldn't they order these kits as well? They said they couldn't and didn't want to be responsible for delayed shipping because they forgot to order the kits. The plant wanted the kits to be ordered automatically, to tie them into the bill of materials for the product. Progress was at a stalemate, so the team gave in to the plant.

The team reluctantly set about adding the kit item number to the bill of materials, but the plant's management said they needed a material specification for the kit *now*. The template for a material specification wasn't designed for something like the kit; it was designed for a raw material, such as wire, plastic, or a printed label. This initiated back-and-forth discussions in numerous meetings as to what should or should not be in the material specification. Questions arose as to how it should look, should there be inspections of incoming material, what would the sampling size be, is the supplier approved, what are the critical inspection points, and so on. And we didn't have resources for extra testing, either.

What started out to simply accommodate the automatic ordering of a shipping kit spiraled out of control to create and approve a material specification and set up sampling plans, incoming inspection training, resources allocation, changes to the bill of materials, and supplier qualifications. Countless meetings and months and months of no activity cost the companies tens of thousands of dollars and a delay in the sample builds of three months. All because a plant didn't want to be responsible for ordering a mundane item, and a person (in trying to get things resolved) offered up a simple solution that ended up being anything but simple. This all could have been avoided if the plant management would have stepped in and directed the local group to handle the ordering as needed.

Is this an exception? Maybe, but the lesson here is twofold.

One, make sure there are clear roles and responsibilities for tasks; and two, scope out a change before implementing to ensure you're fully aware of what it will take to implement. In conducting point two, be sure to reinforce roles and responsibilities.

Let's explore point two a bit further. A management decision was made to replicate operations at a site to another site. Management kept this hush-hush so the assessment of what it would take to transfer the operation was conducted at a high level. (I think you know where this is going.) The decision was made into a project, and the replication was deemed a process transfer. This meant that if everything were to be the same, we would only have to do minimal testing to prove the new site could produce the same as the original site.

That wasn't how it developed. On paper, it did indeed represent a process transfer, meeting the definition as such. However, when digging deeper into the issue, it was found that test methods didn't exist, test methods that *did* exist were not validated, critical dimensions of the component were not defined, and historical performance of the component was not defined. Now, imagine management wanting this process transfer completed within a year. Not likely. The team had to validate the existing test methods, develop and validate the missing test methods, define the missing critical dimensions and validate them, and develop the data to support the historical performance of the component to use to support equivalency of components made at the new site.

This is another example of a snowball effect. In this case, the project assessment failed to identify the inadequacies of the existing process, and a simple project—on paper—turned into a more complicated and involved project. Who had conducted the original assumptions? Yes, management. Again.

Can these things be avoided? Not all the time, but this example points out the need to

- understand the processes you're evaluating;
- be aware of current procedures and requirements; and
- be diligent in researching the pros and cons of a proposal so you can make an informed decision.

This invokes the adage "You cannot judge a book by its cover." Things are sometimes not what they seem. Do not assume, and do not take anything for granted. Confirm, verify, and weigh the options. You will be in a much better position to be successful. It's much easier than standing in front of your management trying to explain why the project will not be done on time or the need for additional money and resources.

36

Baking a Cake

"WOW, THIS CAKE is delicious. Can I have the recipe?" Some companies have multiple locations where they manufacture products or components that go into their products. Sometimes, to protect against catastrophes, the same manufacturing occurs in these sites; this ensures against interruption of product delivery.

Imagine having these multiple sites manufacturing the same product using different specifications or testing raw materials with different methods or requirements. Does that make sense? If something should go wrong, can you compare the data generated from one site to another? Would the product be the same? Of course not.

You just had a slice of the most amazing cake at your best friend's house. You simply *must* have the recipe. Luckily, she's your best friend, and she's more than happy to share the recipe with you.

The following week, you're having company over, so

what better dessert than your friend's cake? The day of your get-together, you carefully measure out all the ingredients and check the oven temperature and time. After the cake has baked and cooled off, you sneak a small piece (no one will notice!) and taste it. Oh my! It tastes just like your friend's!

Now, let's look at this cake analogy and how it relates to manufacturing. There's a successful manufacturing process in one of your locations, but you want to ensure business continuity and protect yourself from natural disaster, political unrest, or worker dissatisfaction. You decide to build a plant elsewhere that will aid in protecting you from these concerns. You recreate the manufacturing process, and all is good. The "cakes" baked at both sites "taste" the same. Over time, however, one of the sites feels it can improve on the recipe and makes changes. Gradually, the two sites diverge in output (cakes).

What happened to your business continuity? It disappeared. You allowed one of the sites to change the recipe (process specification). Then it happens: one of the sites suffers a natural disaster. All is good; you tell management, "We have this covered." You push production on the other plant, and they start supplying "cake" to the downed site's customers. Things are great; the continuity plan worked.

Then something else happens. Slowly and then all at once, the downed site's customers start complaining about the cakes they're getting. Returns and dissatisfied customers are escalating. You allowed the one site to deviate from the recipe; the downed site's customers weren't getting the same cake they were used to getting. You no longer had business continuity. You are making different cakes in taste or looks but calling them the same thing or believing they are the same thing. When the two manufacturing sites were supplying different customers, there were no complaints. Each site's customers were used to the cakes they were getting. When the supplier changed, the expectations were impacted.

I have used this analogy often at work in conversations about material and process specification and differences among multiple locations producing the same thing. At one company I worked at, we had multiple sites manufacturing the "same" items or performing the "same" testing, yet each site had performed differently. Given this incidence, is it possible to have the same outcomes? *No.* Could you compare the different site's data to their test results? *No.* Would the parts perform the same? *No.* The cakes would simply not taste the same.

If your company has multiple sites performing the same tasks or testing, they should be using the same equipment, at best, but they should also be using the same testing or process specifications and controls. This is especially true for material testing. I found it remarkable that our managers and directors—basically management—didn't see this as a significant flaw in our manufacturing processes and, worse, didn't do anything about it. Yet we would get the same failures every year, and the same question would be asked: "How come we have these failures if everything is meeting specifications?"

And the plants? What did they say? They denied they were the problem. "The product meets specification, so it's not us." Do you think anyone checked to see if the difference in specification would still yield a cake that looked and tasted the same? You're right; no one did.

If you're manufacturing the same thing in multiple sites, you need to be using the same recipe, same controls and specifications, and the same equipment, if possible. After all, a gas stove works differently than an electric stove. This is just plain common sense.

You cannot expect to have consistency and maintain the same quality levels at multiple manufacturing sites if you're not diligent in ensuring that all sites perform and act in the same manner. This means management need to be exceedingly diligent in overseeing operational changes and conduct to maintain this consistency.

Let me present some examples from my experiences. A company I worked for decided to open a manufacturing site in Asia. The company transferred manufacturing equipment to the new site, worked out what would be produced, and set up its documentation and process flows. Then management forgot about them. Management walked away. There was no oversight. Then there were problems. Changes were made at the site with incomplete documentation and without valida-tion. The product performance was abysmal.

Problems started coming out of the site with increasing frequency and severity. Management wanted answers. "We need this fixed and now!" was their mantra. "How did this happen?" they asked. The answer was management; they were at fault. Management failed to provide the proper level of oversight, failed to ensure the proper training was in place, and failed to establish proper metrics and accountability. More importantly, management failed to adequately train the new company from the onset and ensure that the training was sustainable. What management decided to do after things got somewhat out of hand was to pull local manufacturing out of the site. If management had made a sincere effort to replicate manufacturing in two Asia plants, the situation would have been different. If management made sure the appropriate training was provided and maintained, these issues wouldn't have arisen. Unfortunately, the site suffered from inadequate instructions and paid the price. Was it the employees' fault?

No, to a large degree it was not, given the minimal instructions and guidance they received. Management expected them to bake the same cake without the proper training and equipment. The site did their best, but it was not good enough.

In another example, a company contracted a vendor to supply a critical product component containing a specific amount of a chemical. The company had specific test methods to follow to ensure the component was dosed correctly. The vendor would test the dose level, find it acceptable, and ship the component to our company, where we would perform the same test to verify the dose level. Yes, you guessed it. The component would fail our test, and we would reject the shipment. We notified the vendor, who naturally was upset. "It passed our testing. How could it fail your testing? You must be doing something wrong."

Things went back and forth between our company and the vendor. Finger-pointing and frustration abounded. The vendor sincerely wanted to get the issue resolved, and of course, so did we. Naturally, we *knew* the vendor was testing wrong, and we actively went about proving it.

The data from the vendor and our company were reviewed, and the test results were compared. In examining our testing data, it appeared there was one technician who consistently had results that were nowhere near the results of the other technicians. It must be that this technician was screwing up; that was the cause of the false positives. After months of investigation, we found the root cause.

The test was very sensitive. We had to take samples and place them into a solution to dissolve the drug to measure the concentration. Through statistical analysis, we found that the step of dissolving the drug had a lot of variation. The amount of fluid we were dissolving the drug in was varying, which was affecting the concentration percentage. To solve this variation, we converted the test from calibrated pipettes to an automated dispensing instrument. This took the human step, consequently the human error, out of the process. The result was a reduction in variation of almost 45 percent. We found that the samples we were failing were actually good! And that technician who had the rogue results? It turned out he was the most accurate and consistent in measuring out the solution; the other technicians were the problem.

This example illustrates the importance of executing processes consistently. You need to make the cake with the exact recipe if you are to stand any chance of having the cake made by different cooks look and taste the same.

Here's another example of baking the cake consistently using the same technique. An internal manufacturing site had been making a component for decades, but it was the sole supplier. To ensure the component supply wouldn't be compromised, the process was introduced into a second plant. Now, this is where things got a bit awkward. The original site supplied all finishing sites, so downstream manufacturing evolved over time to the variation of the components they manufactured. The subtle problem that was overlooked—or, in some cases, exploited—was that the original site had a wide specification for the component, but *they never manufactured components over the full specification range!*

The second site was responsible for validating (proving it could make the component properly) the same component at their site. They had to show their manufactured component was equivalent to the original site. The second site proceeded to go through their validation activities. They tested their component and determined it met specification. All was good, right?

Actually, the new site tested their component at the downstream sites, and their component didn't perform the same as the original site's component. What do you think was done? The new site said their validation was complete because they met specification, and any problems at the downstream sites were their problems.

This is a classic case of myopic decision-making. The second site was only interested in completing their testing/validation, and as long as their component met their specifications, they were satisfied. They didn't care that their customers at the downstream sites wouldn't be able to use their component in the same manner as the original site's component—that was the site's problem. It was done.

Since the original site was around for a very long time, they had set the specification many, many decades ago, but they never tested to see if the specification would work in *all* cases. They were historically producing product at the lower end of the specification, while the second site (the new site) ran at the upper end of the specification. These extremes were different enough to cause problems.

This demonstrates two problems. The first problem was the existing specification didn't reflect what worked or what was working. The downstream sites were used to getting the component at the lower end of the specification, and they built their process around what was consistently provided to them by the original site.

The second problem was the new site didn't consider the historical range of the specification the original site was providing to the downstream sites. If they had done this, they would have had no problem, and everyone would have been happy. The new site's cake was different even though they were using the "same recipe," which wasn't correct. The original site should have changed the specification to reflect what had been historically made. They were not using two cups of sugar, but one cup; if the new site had known this, all would have been peachy.

The fundamental problem underlying all of this is that the original site never wanted to change any specification to which it was required to adhere. Why? Because the larger specification meant they would not have to reject material. Why this attitude? Why didn't these people care about their downstream sites' issues and problems with their component? Because their metrics, set by management, were based on their efficiency and did not make them accountable to downstream problems due to their component. The metrics in place were basically telling the sites, "Here's how I'll measure you," and the sites would say, "Okay, this is what you'll get."

Follow these basic principles for your business:

1. Ensure metrics yield positive behavior. Hold suppliers accountable for efficiency, quality, and performance, especially when dealing with internal operations.

2. Make internal suppliers accountable for internal customers; you do this for external, so why would internal be any different? I have always said that the only difference between internal and external is the first syllable. A company should treat external and internal manufacturers the same.

3. Always review historical performance when establishing a second source. Make sure the cakes will taste the same regardless of who is making them.

4. Hold suppliers accountable for customer performance regarding what they supply and how it is to function. You'll best accomplish this by establishing

specifications *you know* will work under all manufacturing scenarios.

5. Know your processes. Define their optimum run-
    ning parameters and put measures in place to ensure
    they run and stay within these parameters (statistical
    process control), stripping as much as possible from
    reliance on individuals to maintain a process. Make
    the process self-sustaining.

Management should pay attention to what's going on in
their manufacturing sites. First, learn how products are made
and used. There was a time when management rose through
the rank and file and knew its products and manufacturing processes. Unfortunately, those days seem to be bygone.
Management—no one else—is responsible for making sure a
site has what it needs to be successful. Management's issue is it
really doesn't know the products and processes it's managing.
Management itself doesn't know how to bake a cake, so how
can they make the right decisions when it comes to product
quality and consistency?

In these cases, the company's approach was the flaw. In
the end, you can trace a lot of things back to management.
It decides what cake to bake. Actions within a company start
with management decisions and its expectations.

37

Elephants and Jackasses

ONE OF THE most difficult things to recognize and learn how to deal with is politics. There are many types of people in a company. Large corporations hire the best available. They like to hire well-educated, intelligent people. These same hires usually share one trait that made them successful, which in turn makes them dangerous to you due to a competitive nature. This combination of brains and aggression makes for a volatile cocktail of "watch out" for you. These workers want to get ahead, but they want to do it now, not later. They aren't content with "growing" into the job. They want the next promotion ASAP and strategize what it will take to get it.

These highly motivated and talented coworkers are your roadblocks to advancement, and you need to be very careful how you deal with them. If they feel, even remotely, that you may compromise their reputation or their work, then look out. They will make sure you're cut off at your knees. You will rarely win out against them. You need to play their game, and play it better than them, if you can.

You can recognize these people through several traits:

- They typically speak in meetings so you know they are there.
- They volunteer or seek out a role in management's pet projects.
- They aggressively seek out high-visibility projects.
- They organize and run volunteer programs for the extra credit in public relations exposure it provides.

Early in their careers, they embraced the understanding of perception. They dress professionally at all times and are always reserved in their manners and behavior around co-workers, especially management. You will recognize them. They will be the ones who sit in the front rows at meetings or hover close to management in gatherings.

They are not all bad people, but they have a very focused game plan and you don't want to be in their way. That isn't acceptable to them, and it will not be pleasant for you. So be aware and be advised. I tried to identify them early. I would look to see what they were pursuing as career moves and determine if it would affect my goals. If so, then I had to accept that I was in for a fight. Did I want the job badly enough to go against them? That's what you need to ask yourself.

Politics can have a broader interpretation than just observing the type of people in a company. The size of a company and the type of ownership create different cultures in a general sense. I found that company size *does* impact your ability to grow.

Small Companies

Families, or a group of owners, usually own small companies. Working in a small company will give you a lot of flexibility, which will be limited by your ambitions and capability. However, moving up in the organization and getting a higher salary will be limited. Management is usually off-limits, reserved for the family or close friends. How well the company does depends on the owner or owners and their business savvy.

But the benefit of a small company is that it's typically flexible and versatile, which allows you to perform different jobs at the same time. Small companies can adapt quickly to changes as long as it doesn't entail a huge investment. This is a great way to learn different skill sets and expand your experience. However, the stability of a small company can be iffy. You're at the mercy of the owner's talent to procure orders and to survive through downturns in orders. You do need to be aware when there's a transition of ownership to siblings. Siblings don't often continue the track record. They aren't as committed to the business, or sometimes running the business is not their forte. Remember, they got the job through their family connection, not necessarily through their business acumen or skills. This is another version of not learning the products or processes for which management has responsibility.

Medium-Size Companies

Medium-size companies are like hybrids of small and large companies. They can blend the best of both worlds. They're still relatively small enough to be adaptable and flexible, but they also have the resources to sustain themselves through business downturns and to adapt to market changes.

You'll tend to have more flexibility than in a large company, but not as much as in a small company. Career growth is typically better as medium-size companies can be more competitive with salaries and benefits than a small company. They can still be family-owned or governed by a group, so movement into management may still be limited.

Large Companies

The good and the bad collide. Most large companies have been established for a long time and have high visibility with the public. They are very much aware of their brand or identity and protect it. Jobs tend to be very well-defined, and advancement is defined through a more formal program that outlines the skills and qualifications needed for positions of increasing responsibilities. Politics is very well-defined, and you benefit if you can plug into it early on. However, politics makes it difficult to get hired; you need to have an "in" with its network so you have someone pulling for you to get hired. You may not have the ability to move around as much; for example, if you're in finance, then you stay in finance. It's possible but not easy to move between disciplines in a large company.

Large companies tend to have systems in place that have been adapted over time. These adaptions may have been poorly or effectively executed. If poorly (as where I worked), then the bureaucracy of the standing systems creates very defined roles and responsibilities. This structure translates into jobs to administer the system rather than to advance the company.

I could go on describing the main differences, but I think providing a table would make it easier to see how (generally speaking) small, medium-size, and large company advantages can affect your career.

	SMALL	MEDIUM	LARGE
WORKFORCE	Small	Small to modest	Large
FLEXIBILITY TO CHANGE	High (asset-dependent?)	Medium (asset-dependent)	Low (has assets, but lacks flexible systems)
JOB FLEXIBILITY	High	Medium	Low (specific roles and very territorial)
COMPANY STABILITY	Low (usually very little reserves)	Medium	High (large reserves that allow weathering through long, difficult times)
SALARY	Low (difficult to attract talent)	Medium	High (can demand the best people, which means they will pay more for skills and talent—and can afford to)
ADVANCEMENT	Low (typically family or partnerships are in the way)	Medium	High
BENEFITS	Low	Medium	High
USE OF LATEST TECHNOLOGY	Low to high	Medium to high	High
POLITICS	Low (family or between owners)	Medium (mainly between owners and network)	High (all kinds)
OPERATING SYSTEMS	Low to high	Medium to high	Medium to high
DIVERSITY	Low	Medium to high	High
Job Security	Low to medium	Medium to high	Low to medium
WORKER EMPATHY (toward the company)	Low to high	Medium to high	Medium to high

38

Communication Constipation

I'VE WORKED AT several companies over my career, and what I find the most fascinating and frustrating is the lack of clear lines of communication as organizations grow larger. For example, in a large corporation, the management may desire that something be done by the end of the month (i.e., in twenty business days). They, in turn, instruct their direct reports to do it in fifteen business days, as they don't want it to be late. Then this level repeats the same thing in the same manner, and now it's due in ten days. The next level states the due date is five days, and finally it's communicated to you that management has this crisis and it needs to be done by the end of the week. See how the many levels of communication—poor communication, at that—turned a simple request into a panic for the lower managerial levels who are now scrambling to fulfill this emergency need?

This same scenario happens with projects that are given shortened deadlines with no rational reason provided. The dilemma is that the project team will communicate that they need either more resources or money or encountered issues that need more time to be resolved. Does middle management communicate this upward? Not really. They will vacillate around with the issue, saying things like the following:

- "We're on time."
- "We'll be on time. Don't worry."
- "There are some issues, but we're addressing them."

One big reason this can occur is that management gets filtered updates. There's a lack of transparency between project teams and their problems and what management is told, which is typical. You see this in monthly updates all the time. The direct reports provide details on what's going on with their projects, but management distills this down into brief summaries, eliminating potential issues, and passes on their updates. Then the next level of management does the same. And so on and so on until management gets a very sanitized update that makes things appear like they are wonderfully rosy.

If communications were done transparently and management were more engaged, then more realistic decisions and timing could occur. One can never overcommunicate when it comes to critical issues and functions. More importantly, ensure that all parties understand the information conveyed. Large companies need to develop better, unfiltered lines of communication. This is best achieved by reducing the number of management levels. If there are too many levels, then the organizational structure is inadequate and inefficient.

Companies   should   reevaluate   their   managerial infrastructure as they grow to ensure it's optimal for what they're trying to accomplish. Sadly, companies often just cobble together patches onto existing antiquated systems or purchase new customizable systems, but then balk at the costs associated with customizing. They end up putting in systems "upgrades" that are just as painful to operate as the systems they were intended to replace.

Companies should reinvent their management structure just as much as they reinvent their products. That doesn't mean adding layers of management. It means maintaining the most efficient layers of management so communication is not garbled. Middle management should be held accountable for uncommunicated delays and for adequately resourcing projects. Good management sees beyond the horizon and knows how to balance risk at the appropriate time and to the appropriate degree.

Bear this in mind if you get into a position of management. Ensure the right information and the right message are communicated upward. Avoid creating additional management levels. Rather, look for ways to adapt your management structure to accommodate your growing needs.

Soapbox Perspectives

Advice is a double-edged sword. On the one hand, you have insightful advice that is very helpful and makes one pause to reflect and consider. On the other hand, advice can easily become the rants and raves of a questionable mind. The following chapters reflect the latter.

39

Management and Awareness

I'm sure you've done the following while growing up. You come across a lake or a large body of water. There's no wind, and the water's surface is like a mirror, with barely a ripple. You pick up a stone and throw it out into the middle and watch the small geyser of water as the stone plunges into the water and sinks to the bottom. Waves form and race away from the point of entry, expanding the farther they travel. The waves also get smaller and smaller until they disappear.

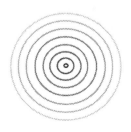

This is a perfect analogy of bureaucracy and its effectiveness. Freeze the moment. You're now looking at concentric rings that ripple less and less the farther they flow from where the stone plunged into the water. Now picture each ripple as a layer of management and the height of the wave as that layer of management's knowledge of the processes and products for which it feels responsible. The higher the ripple or wave, the more knowledgeable that layer of management is about the product or manufacturing. Think of the process as the center where the stone landed in the water. Notice as you move farther away from the process, the weaker the ripples or waves become. The smaller the height of the waves, the less knowledgeable management is because of how removed they are from the process. This is typically what happens as you add more layers of management. The less interaction a management layer has with actual manufacturing, the lesser its knowledge of the process, and the more susceptible the decisions are to be wrong or skewed away from the center.

A successful company has effective management due to one of two things:

- It has minimized the layers so there's a reasonable interaction/awareness of production issues; or
- The management has an effective program that balances promotion up through the ranks while also bringing in people from outside.

Those promoted through the ranks have demonstrated product and process knowledge, not simply "held the job." Those hired from outside have proven themselves in like manner but bring complementary skills and insights.

There's the argument that well-educated people can learn anything, which may be true, but they need to be brought in at a point where they can either learn the product and processes or provide active training. How can anyone make decisions on something he or she knows nothing about? Would you hire people to run your business if they didn't know your policies, product, or business strategies? You cannot expect someone from the outside to make the right decision all the time. You need a balance between two extremes: experiences gained by rising through the ranks and outside hires. It's like what I said earlier in this book: in a good financial portfolio, you have both conservative investments (internal advancements) and aggressive investments (external hires).

Unfortunately nowadays, some managers take the position that a person who must learn the product and processes to manage is just as effective as someone who has the experience. But the former is really just managing procedures. There's no real thinking involved. How can that person make informed decisions without sufficient knowledge of the product or processes to make the right decisions?

Yes, we should follow procedures, but knowledge of the product and processes is an important element that shouldn't be ignored. Unfortunately, product and process knowledge is no longer valued. If it were valued, would it not condemn those who are hired from outside? Of course it would. But large companies feel that's the desired way to grow. People brought in from outside infuse new ideas and new ways, but these need to be tempered with product and process knowledge so the right steps and decisions are made that don't disrupt manufacturing or cost monies.

In a company I worked at, the president had started out in manufacturing. The vice president of manufacturing worked

his way up from manufacturing. These balanced board members who were brought in from the outside. Decisions were
spot-on when it came to product strategies and changes. There
was a cohesive balance between product and process knowledge and ideas and techniques from the outside, and how
these were applied to make them effective and meaningful.
Nowadays, outside ideas are applied thinking one size fits
all and what works somewhere else will work here without
considering the complexity of product manufacturing lines
and structures. If large companies are going to maintain their
success, they need to take the following steps:

- acknowledge experience
- value experience
- balance their intellectual portfolio
- balance experience with outside ideas

What's needed more and more is management's willing-
ness to dirty its hands. That means learning the business
before taking on roles of responsibility. Those willing to do
so should also secure a long-term investment commitment
from management. Unfortunately, we live in a here-and-now
world. *What have you done for me lately without long-term investment
in our people resources?* It's like putting your portfolio into short-
term bonds but nothing with long-term growth. Sink or swim
by the moment. In some cases, management is promoted
or switched around (as part of their development) so they
will not be in the same role when the fallout from their bad
decision needs to be fixed. They should be held accountable
for their programs. One example of this is when someone in
management develops a new idea to integrate into the business and then moves on to another position. What happens

next? Just as the idea goes into implementation, it is a *disaster*. What is done? The management that requested this initiative has been promoted as a result of said idea and is no longer around. The new management is left to try to make it work. This usually means it is replaced with the next new idea and hopes it's better.

A company I worked at had a mission statement that was taken very seriously. Each year, we had to answer question after question on how the company and our management behaved and followed the mission statement. If there were questions that received a low score, then a task team was made accountable to fix them and fix them immediately.

Boy, how times do change. Flash forward a number of years, when the mission statement survey came around again. We all answered the questions honestly, as we were very frustrated by the way the department was run and by the general direction of our projects. Well, that was a bad idea! Our department received the lowest score in the company. *Finally*, we thought, *things will be addressed!*

Yes, they were addressed all right.

Management was angry that they were put under the spotlight for the lowest scores. Management set about fixing the problem by laying off personnel, restructuring, and cutting back on resources for projects. The vice president at the time was a great guy from marketing. He was filling in and told us that we were idiots for answering the survey truthfully. All we succeeded in doing was attracting management's attention, and how did that work out for us?

Our vice president moved on shortly after that, and we got a new one to break in. The next survey came around, and we basically fudged our answers. When the results came back, you would have thought the vice president had just saved the world. His grin was so wide you would have thought the top half of his head would fall back. Our department went from the worst to the best in a year. (And of course, the vice president took all the credit for it.)

The mission statement survey went from a viable tool for the company that made management accountable to more of a marketing tool. In my opinion, this was mainly due to the insolating position management took concerning the product and employees. Management's focus was more on perception and ensuring they always looked favorable. If you were brought in from the outside, did you really value a survey? After all, the mission statement was a great public relations tool. It made us a feel-good company; it was great public relations, a truly beautiful thing. If only management took the survey answers seriously—and for what they were intended. Would everything really be so bad if they did?

Unfortunately, this seems to be modern business.

Self-Sustaining Systems

I often wonder why corporations need so many layers. Management will tell you it's due to the size and complexity of the business. However, a company needs to redesign itself as it grows. Systems and procedures need to be challenged. The organization needs to think outside the box and put procedures in place that will work for the future state of the business. Procedures need to be self-sustaining and not reliant on specific individuals. A self-sustaining system allows for a reduction in skill set to manage the system. This approach falls in line with the increasing use of contractors and outside hiring rather than promoting through internal development.

As companies evolve, so should the systems they use. I worked at a company where the systems had been modified and cobbled together over many years to accommodate changes in government regulations and international requirements. Did the company redesign their systems for today? No. And what was the result of these patchwork procedures? It took over eighteen months for us to make a product change. *Let that sink in.* A company operating using procedures that allowed component changes to get completed in a year and a half. Do you think management would redesign such systems? Is eighteen months the benchmark for an industry? Does this allow the company to be responsive? No, but the company had been doing it this way for years.

I tried to redesign it. I worked with one of the engineers, and we had a proposal that would get us to three months. Unfortunately, management declined to adopt the proposal. Management was so far removed from the process and knew so little about the process that they didn't see the need and could not recognize the need. The sad part is the real issue is that most managers don't want to rock the boat until they get their inevitable promotion, and then it's no longer their problem—apparently just not in their metrics. Couple this with a plethora of contractors who are just doing what they're told, and you see the recipe for incompetence and inadequacy from miles away.

A Challenge for America

I challenge industries to challenge *themselves* to start requiring management to know what they're managing, to ensure management is a good mix of outside and inside experience. Management needs to redesign systems to be more efficient and effective. This should also reduce the layers of management, making a company more profitable. US industry must realize that if the United States is to really be competitive in a global world, systems should be enabling, not disabling.

Just consider the television show that disguises company management so they can see firsthand how the business is working and what the workers are thinking. In no show that I have seen did the person in disguise have any idea how their programs were working or even how to do the simplest task in the operation. This is such a sad commentary on American industry. I find the show to be a great example of how management is oblivious to how its "program of the month" or its company structure is what is affecting company vitality. In almost every show, the workers lack the proper training and equipment or are not treated like an important part of the company. American industry needs to realize that people make a company. The workers are the company. It's the employees who generate ideas that can reduce waste and can make the company successful. American industry needs to invest in infrastructure improvements and new technology, but they also need to invest in their most precious resource—their people.

Here is another analogy. Look at management as driving a car, with the car symbolizing the company. What does the driver do? The driver (management) looks where the car is heading and is taking (leading) the car where management wants the company to go. The driver plans the route and timing. Good drivers use their rear-facing mirrors (where the company is now and the status of their passengers or workers) while they're driving. They don't solely look ahead.

This is the same in business. Management needs to keep an eye on the current business while leading the company

forward. Management cannot simply use cruise control and ignore where they are or where they were. Management needs to
be just as aware of the current state of the business as what the
future business of the company will be. This awareness needs
to be more than just receiving reports. They need to know,
really know, what's going on internally with their company as
much as leading the company forward. Are the metrics truly
accurate? Are the reports accurately reflecting the state of the
business's efficiency and effectiveness? Not paying adequate
attention to the base business—which is fueling the company's growth—may be another reason why management does
not fix things.

So why won't management fix things? Here are a few
possible reasons:

1. They don't realize a system is broken because
   a. they have little product or process knowledge to
      recognize the problem;
   b. they don't see process problems as something
      that has to be addressed;
   c. they don't want to address glitches (because they
      won't affect their bonuses); or
   d. the mistakes have no direct impact on manage-
      ment's everyday role.
2. The issue at hand isn't something that's getting negative visibility in the company.
3. The system seems to be working, so what's wrong?
   Nobody is complaining from where the managers sit.
4. Their thinking is shortsighted, with only short-term
   goals.
5. The company lacks long-term planning goals for internal infrastructure and systems.

6. They are making money, so they don't understand what the problem is.
7. The issue isn't easy to measure or obvious to quantify the cost.

Hopefully, if management can

- incorporate a short-term and long-term investment approach,
- get more involved in becoming knowledgeable about their products and manufacturing processes, and
- encourage management job stability, then ...

American industry will be in a better position to be viable and a thriving world producer and provider. Sure, it takes re-evaluation of how a company operates and accountability, but if larger profits, success, and growth are the result, why not?

40

Metes and Bounds; Roles and Responsibilities

I WORKED WITH a person who was very dedicated to her job. If she saw something wasn't done right, she fixed it. She'd even do work that was the responsibility of other employees. This is a commendable attitude, but there's a drawback to it. If you're thorough and need to ensure everything is right to the point of redoing or doing others' work, then what happens? You're so busy doing their work that *your* work suffers. That's what happened to this person. She was so dedicated to her responsibility that she could not, in good conscience, let the inadequate or subpar work of others affect her work. While it was a noble approach and attitude, it didn't help her. The work that was her responsibility suffered, and she fell woefully behind. This caused a performance concern for her. Given that she was very dedicated and wanted to be sure everything was done correctly, how could she accomplish this without damaging herself in the effort?

There's a win-win solution for all, and it accomplishes the same results. Why did the poet Robert Frost say that good fences make good neighbors? Because there was an agreed-upon demarcation of where the property line was. Without a doubt, there was the fence; therefore, this side was mine, and that side was yours. The same principle applies here. If my coworker had made it clear to the project manager whose responsibilities were whose, then the project manager could have made sure the prerequisite work my coworkers needed was done correctly so she did not have to do the work. Timelines would be accountable to the appropriate person, and all would be addressed. It would take intervention by her manager to ensure the project leader addressed her concerns, but it could be done.

If you do others' jobs for them, they do not learn. They also get the impression that *you're* responsible for the jobs, not them. It's like the adage "Feed a person a fish, and you feed them for a day. Teach a person to fish, and you feed them for a lifetime." In actuality, you're doing the person a disservice. Doing work for others hinders their job growth. They don't learn how to do the job and develop as a resource.

Sometimes the best thing to do is the hardest. You need to allow a person to work through issues to develop responsibilities. You need to refrain from doing the actual work. Mentor him or her and provide constructive feedback, but don't do the work. If you have a good rapport with the person's manager, you can also have the manager be a mentor and review the work as it progresses. You need your time to do your work, not someone else's. So be mindful of your needs and don't let the needs of others cloud your responsibilities.

41

Accountability

I REMEMBER BACK in the nineties when team concept was becoming the new way of handling projects. Most comments settled around the same thing—no one person will be accountable. We were so used to working independently, with the project leader coordinating the team. Remember, this was before conference calls and web conferencing. You did your part, and the project leader handled how the project went together as well as any next steps. We saw the team member approach as a way to dodge responsibility and accountability. Blame would be on the team rather than the individual. But where was the accountability?

With changing technology, team-based projects became the norm. The whole blame-the-team mentality is now the way of business. There's a lot of victim thinking:

- "I cannot meet at that time."

- "I had other commitments."
- "I wasn't given clear instructions."

You get the idea.

There was an individual in my department who didn't attend an early-morning team meeting. The meeting was held because the project leader was based in Europe. The individual said he had family obligations, which was why he couldn't come in early. He said he came in between 8:00 and 8:30 a.m. In reality, he came in between 8:30 and 9:00 a.m. You would think he would try to get in at 8:00 a.m. to attend the second half of the meeting, but he wouldn't even try. This was once a week. He didn't even tell the project leader he couldn't make the meeting. There was no ownership. So where was this person's sense of responsibility?

His attitude should have been, "I own this, and I am responsible."

There's No "I" in "Team" (But There Should Be)

Early in my career, if you were called onto the carpet and chewed out, it was reflected in your review, or in worse situations, you were fired. Nowadays, it's not your fault. I put the blame for this vagary squarely on management.

The lack of accountability and ownership is the big issue with today's business philosophy. I have seen a director require something to be done in a new project. Before it's fully implemented, he moves on to another job. And guess what? The new program fails. But the director has another job, so he's not held accountable.

If industry is going to be successful, there needs to be a return to accountability and ensuring initiatives are completed before someone can take on a new position or role. If management were held accountable in this manner, then teams would also be held accountable as the success of management now depends on the success of the teams. With accountability comes responsibility.

It's not uncommon for team members to change throughout a project. Often, there will be very few original team members left when the project is completed and launched. This is disruptive to team continuity and project efficiency. The original team members know the ins and outs of the development phase and the issues to be addressed and how issues were resolved. When you cycle through people, this information is potentially lost. It's preferable to maintain team members throughout the life cycle of a project, until the project is completed. This is difficult to do, but if it could be encouraged and managed through some form of reward system, that would be ideal for teams.

The downside of teams is a lack of accountability. This is the downside of utilizing teams. Teams can diffuse accountability in a way that there are no repercussions for poor performance—it was the team. Management needs to be aware of this dilemma. Teams work, but there needs to be a defined accountability within the team to sustain positive individual performance of team members.

There was a project that was launched that was a collaboration between two companies. A misfunction was noticed during development, but it was discounted by the lead company even after the support company repeatedly brought the misfunction to the lead company's attention. The product was launched despite the protestations. Soon, field complaints started being reported. Users were experiencing the misfunction that was found by the support company. Sales dropped significantly enough that the product was dropped. When the end-of-the-year bonus time came, all team members received a significantly lower bonus. All team members were indiscriminately punished. The team from the support company was furious. After all, they had repeatedly pointed the issue out to the lead company, who disregarded their concern. How did accountability work in this scenario? Not very well. Those who should have been held accountable were punished by the reduced bonus, but so were the team members who had no control over the outcome.

This is a good example of how individual accountability within a team needs to be defined to ensure employee performance meets company expectations. This type of accountability can only be driven by management.

42

Corporate Entropy

ONE DAY I was reading a book on entropy, which is a scientific term for the idea that everything eventually goes from order to disorder, and I thought how this could apply to what I was seeing at work. Therefore, *corporate entropy*.

Over the years, I have noticed that as an organization grows larger and larger, it doesn't seem possible to sustain itself at the same level of efficiency and quality. This, to me, is corporate entropy. Successful organizations are such because they were created and became successful due to the tenacity, insight, dedication, and knowledge of their founders, along with their ability to attract good people.

What happens over a long period of successful growth is complacency. Management relaxes its values, falls back on its reputation, and reduces the emphasis on training and internal promotion. This—along with the growth of its bureaucracy—expands its inefficiency. Promoting upward from within and from manufacturing ranks becomes minimal or obsolete over time as management hires friends from external companies. The solid structure in place starts to break down. Costs fluctuate, and projects develop flaws, which leads to poor results, with missed launch dates. Changes are mistakes that are costly. There's little or no transfer of knowledge from those retiring to those who may be promising employees. New management from outside has no knowledge of the subtleties of the product and manufacturing processes. Couple this with the dilution of knowledge due to the increased use of external contractors replacing full-time employees.

Remember that a company spends a lot of time training contract employees only to have them leave for another contract or that coveted full-time position. They take all that training and knowledge with them, notwithstanding the disruption to the projects they were supporting. A significant reduction in loyalty occurs, along with a reduction in accountability and responsibility. Therefore, corporations become failures; it's why their competitors can overtake them, why lawsuits against their products increase and profits decline. When complaints increase, government fines can become more common. This is a problem in US industry. It is affecting age-old companies that lost their roots, lost their hunger, lost their expertise, lost their focus, and lost their identity. It is unfortunate, but reality. Management's role in all this? It is the root cause of this entropy. Management is more focused on shareholder expectations, thus the fixation on short-term deliverables, completely ignoring long-term positioning. Instead of long-term company stability, management's main concern seems to be maneuvering for that next promotion, profit margins, and dividends.

I truly find it sad seeing the indifference and complacency that are permeating and degrading companies. As part of management, you're responsible for the vitality of the company. Does making $10,000,000 versus $9,800,000 really make a difference if that difference was used to ensure proper training and proper transfer of knowledge and to maintain core full-time employees to avoid knowledge loss? As management, this is your responsibility. I truly hope the short-term mentality of US industry comes to recognize the need to also have a long-term commitment to training and preserving core competency and a core workforce.

Future Investment

As in an investment portfolio, you invest in short-term, aggressive programs and long-term, low-yield programs as a balance or hedge against severe fluctuations. This creates a balanced portfolio, which provides good solid growth over time.

Now let's look at a portfolio that's mainly short-term, high-yield investments. This is akin to a company hiring contractors and external management with no emphasis on internal promotions. Your short-term achievements may be realized, but then you find quality errors and oversights that cost you in customer satisfaction and customer loyalty—and even allow competition to make inroads into your market share. Your complaint-handling departments swell in size, and the back-end costs rise. This happens to a lot of large companies, but they don't seem to be concerned because they're hitting their shareholder and market metrics. That's what it's all about. Besides, since management isn't held accountable in the long term—since managers are promoted often within a three-year window—they aren't around to take the hit. Someone else would be responsible for cleaning up the mess, but with victim think as the issue, it's not management's fault, so it's not held accountable, either. It sees the writing on the wall and looks to get out ASAP.

I remember a conversation with the vice president of quality and the need to have standard documentation if we were truly going to operate as a global manufacturing engine. I still recall his blank stare as I explained why this was important. When I was finished, he replied, "These are very good points. Thank you." That was all.

No surprise when I found out two weeks later that he was promoted to another role. America has become inefficient and indifferent to quality. There's a basic lack of responsibility and naivety toward quality. Building quality up front is cheaper than the cost to address quality issues after the fact. The problem with most companies in regard to this issue is a lack of the ability to quantify their costs postconsumer. If companies would place value on infrastructure and people hours spent to address consumer quality, they would see that they have the opportunity to increase their profits. Infuse a bit more quality control into manufacturing processes and hold management accountable. These simple changes are impossible to implement given today's business philosophies. Shortsighted thinking and planning costs more in the end.

43

The Cost of Quality— Not If, But When

YOU WILL NEED to pay for quality. What management needs to decide is *when* they will pay for it. This is a crucial decision and not an easy one for a lot of companies. There are two ways you can pay for quality—before or after. Let's start with the before—by far the hardest to justify.

Quality before means you build quality into the manufacturing process. You put inspections prior to the process becoming instable before transferring to the next process step. You establish sampling plans to ensure you meet the alpha risk (producer's risk—the risk that you reject something that's acceptable) and beta risks (consumer's risk—the risk of accepting something that's actually defective) you can tolerate.

This is the desired approach in manufacturing, but herein lies the problem with management: a company cannot quantify the losses they avoided by implementing quality up front.

They cannot really quantify the cost of lawsuits they avoided, the replacement product they had to eat, the loss in customers due to product dissatisfaction, or the cost of loss product that could have been potentially sold. They could potentially factor in the costs avoided by not having to fund a huge department to handle customer complaints. Sure, they will need such a department, but it wouldn't take tons of people to run it.

In this approach, management only sees the cost or expenses lost to sampling, rejection, process corrections, retraining, and so on, which are the normal factors associated with quality. Sure, these controls cost money, and yes, occasionally a process will make a bad product. (In a normal distribution, it would be considered acceptable for three samples to be outliers out of one hundred.) This is the cost of doing business the right way. But what's the alternative?

The flip side is to reduce your quality controls (management looks at this as an opportunity to save money). This means reducing sample size, eliminating when samples are taken, and reducing defect classifications. I see this happening in businesses more and more. Quality is taking a back seat. I had a plant manager tell me that a component dimension wasn't critical because "no one complains about it so we don't need to measure it." Nice thing to say, especially when the plant manager wasn't an expert on the component or responsible for it. In this approach to quality, management sees only the loss in measurable devices/components that could have been made into a product. But what are they missing in this myopic viewpoint? Management sees the cost savings in reducing sampling and rejection criteria, but the significant areas they fail to acknowledge are the cost of all those things we discussed before that couldn't be measured—the cost of lawsuits, the cost of replacement product, the loss in customers due to product dissatisfaction, and the cost of loss product that could have been potentially sold.

These areas are now increasing due to poor quality. Complaint departments and support personnel grow larger as more people are needed to handle complaints. Handling complaints and product defects is far costlier than implementing quality in manufacturing. The cost of management meetings to "discuss" market failures and how to manage public perception. The cost to gather market complaint data and the loss in available resources (manufacturing support, operators, research and development) to "fix" the product problems drain on a company's productivity. These problems are overlooked and unquantified but are impacting a company's bottom line. In some cases, management accepts these losses as the cost of doing business and do not feel they can change them. Are there any metrics a company uses to track these losses? No, but some companies track their time frames to close out corrections, only because in some fields the government pays attention to these issues. If the government wasn't looking into them, companies wouldn't either.

What I am saying is that companies fail repeatedly to understand that it's cheaper to factor in quality *up front* rather than afterward. I've seen this play out time and again. In a company I worked at, a particular plant took pride in all their inspectors. They had rooms filled with inspectors checking components before they were passed on for further processing. Is this a cost savings? No, it's not. Think how it would be if they designed and structured their processes not to *make* defects so they wouldn't need to inspect in quality. They should be using visual inspection systems and robust processes, putting in precise controls, and training, training, training their operators.

Quality cannot be avoided. You need to pay for quality. It's a decision you need to make—pay up front (which is, in the long run, cheaper) or pay later (and pay dearly).

If I were to summarize the importance of quality to manufacturing, I would have to combine it with other areas I have spoken about and state, from my experience, that success lies in following ETQ.

E Stands for Experience

You need to preserve and pass on experience. Experience is often hard-earned and earned often through blood, sweat, and tears, as they say. The most valuable experience comes from failures. What company can afford to repeat mistakes of the past?

Companies need to develop ways to document the experience of their senior workforce before they leave or retire. When they leave or retire, their knowledge goes with them. It is these senior employees who often know the fix to problems that they often fix without anyone being aware. If companies do not document this knowledge, then significant resources and time are lost trying to fix problems that could have been fixed quickly and with less cost. This loss time and resources could have focused on growth projects rather than base business corrective actions.

It's disappointing to see how companies are allowing well-qualified and experienced employees to retire or leave for other reasons. Experienced employees tend to get frustrated when their company makes decisions based on costs and not quality, minimizing their concerns for the consumer. Experienced employees often are overlooked for promotions, with companies preferring to promote their younger workforce. Companies may not want their younger workforce to leave, but they need experienced employees too. The sad thing is that companies are not valuing experience anymore—it's all about hiring entry-level workers or using contractors. ("Hey, they are cheaper, and we can hire two for one! What a deal!")

What management is ignoring is that whole thing called experience. Those seasoned employees are helping you avoid repeating mistakes of the past; they're a balancing perspective for evaluating new ideas. Those "old employees" are good to have around to train the new employees. Unfortunately, companies don't use these old employees for that; they prefer to push them out, marginalize them, or give them poor ratings to frustrate them into retiring.

It's sad to see this happening. Companies are losing expertise by the year. I sit in meetings, and almost all the people in the meeting have been with the company fewer than five years, never worked in manufacturing, and could not identify a product if they saw it. But these same people are making what they think are cost-saving and clever solutions. As an older employee, I convey concerns, but my concerns are discounted as not relevant. Management's position is that it's more important to hit that target date and *make more money*! So there are complaints. *Oh, only one serious accident caused by our product? That's not bad, right? I mean, look at all we sell. Statistically we are still awesome! And we have factored into our metrics that you will be done by such and such a date, so do not fail me!*

The experienced employee helps companies do it right, do it well, and temper the drive to market with knowledge and experience to check for quality issues and potential performance flaws that could affect the product. The experienced employee trains the new employees on the history of product, processes, and so on. After all, companies evolved manufacturing processes from issues that occurred, which translate into experience. Picture the old employees as walking histories of your products and processes. They have information you can't learn in school, can't download off the internet, and can't hire from outside (if you make proprietary products).

I hope this trend can be arrested and the pendulum stops swinging away from valuing experience.

T Stands for Training

Training is proportional to your process complexity and human reliance. The more a process's quality and efficiency are controlled/reliant on human interaction, the higher the risk of defects, failures, and delays. Training needs to be ongoing. Also, it shouldn't rely on one operator training another. Ever hear of the game "Whisper Down the Lane"? In the game, people line up, and the first person in line whispers a phrase to another so no one else hears what is said. That person then does the same to the next person in line, and so on until the last person in line is told the phrase. The last person then repeats what was whispered to them out loud. The funny outcome of this game is how garbled the phrase gets between what the first person said compared to what the last person in the line said. In whispering the phrase repeatedly, the phrase is corrupted by each person's ability to remember and repeat the phrase. The more complicated the phrase, the more likelihood the phrase will be corrupted.

This same phenomenon happens when operators train operators. Bad habits and shortcuts are passed on, and training efficacy is compromised. The ideal state is to have designated trainers who, in turn, are reviewed to ensure they are consistent among themselves.

Training via a program where you have employees read a document as a way of training is worthless. The only positive is you can show metrics regarding on-time training. How do you confirm the trainee (reader of the document taking the training) understands the document? How do you know the trainee will retain the information? What does a trainee do if there's a question? This form of training isn't effective and is only a metrics-driven methodology.

Q Stands for Quality

Unfortunately, quality is often misapplied and vilified as a consumer of profits and not a positive aspect to manufacturing. As I mentioned, pay now or pay later. Too many companies spend a dime to save a nickel and don't even know they're doing so. They believe they're generating cost savings when they're really losing profits due to consumer dissatisfaction, returns, litigation, and stalled consumer growth.

If a company were to focus on these three areas of ETQ, it should be a sustainable, viable organization for quite some time. It comes down to choices—choices made by management. See how this all comes back to management? If management is hands-on—aware of product/processes so right decisions are made—the company will be heading in the right direction.

Success comes down to management and its strengths and weaknesses. If managers are dedicated and focused, you should be fine. Otherwise, management is just milking the cow for its own benefit, which translates into short-term goals.

If I can convey to you one thing to always keep in the back of your mind as you advance in your career, it's that quality comes at a price, no matter what. The thing you need to decide is *when* you want to pay for it.

A Brief History Lesson

Quality was a big issue with Japanese products after World War II. The quality of Japanese products was laughable. Japan knew they needed to do something and set about to address the issue. Statistical control was embraced and implemented into manufacturing, and slowly Japan's quality improved. The result is that most people in the United States generally view Japanese goods as having superior quality to America's manufactured goods.

The difference was Japan infused quality into its manufacturing processes to ensure goods produced would be of the highest possible quality. Did this add cost? Of course, but this was offset by increased sales. Because quality was built in and product performed better and lasted longer, consumers were willing to pay *more*! With quality built in, fewer costs were incurred postmanufacturing. The net result was more profits overall, increased market share, and brands identified with quality and value, which is a benefit that aids in selling more product.

Do you think if Japan continued to focus more on cost and ignored quality that it would have ended up in the same position it's in today? Of course not. Quality drives profit. You do not achieve quality by

- meeting deadlines at all costs,
- funding huge customer complaint centers,
- replacing defective goods through loss revenue, and
- making up for defective components that consume capacity through additional manufacturing demands.

At some point in your career, you'll need to make tough decisions with project deadlines and management ultimatums. I was in a position once with a project where we needed to deliver a machine by a date that was basically arbitrarily set. The machine wasn't working right, so I delayed delivery until things were made right. I reasoned that it was better to have the machine at the manufacturer than to try to get the manufacturer to come to our site for the repairs. Several months later, we received the machine with all the changes and modifications completed. The machine worked well. The funny thing was no one remembered that we were late in delivery because the machine was working. Imagine what would have been the case if we had shipped it and it wasn't working. Sometimes it's better to ask forgiveness than to meet someone else's expectations without delivering all that was expected.

In the situation above, I made sure the quality was there. I wasn't indifferent to the deadline, but it was more important that the machine worked when received. With anything you do, weigh the risks and rewards. It's especially important when in situations like the one above to manage expectations very closely and provide very clear objectives. I would rather have it right and late than early and wrong.

44

Training

TRAINING IS VITALLY important if our US industry wants to remain viable. Contractors are the trend, but contractors have less allegiance to a company than an employee getting benefits. Training contractors may not have a lasting benefit.

I understand the need for contractors, but businesses are utilizing contractors to reduce direct overhead that can potentially have disastrous results in terms of retained expertise. Companies need to realize that if they want to augment their workforce with contractors, they must maintain a core competency of full-time employees. This is essential to pass on hard-earned experience to a stable workforce and preserve product and process knowledge. These are keys to maintaining a company's vitality and stability.

If management doesn't view training as value added, then long term a company suffers. If management were to state that training is important and learning the business is critical to good management and a company's vitality, then they wouldn't be able to justify nepotism without training. Some companies accept nepotism—to bring in friends or their network people from the outside and put them into positions of responsibility. The company's friends just jump in, and management tells them to keep doing so and so and you'll be fine. They may say, "You'll learn the ropes as you go." This is concerning as bad decisions and strategies can be implemented without the benefit of product and process knowledge.

This reminds me of a joke about monkeys I heard a long time ago. It's a good analogy about why we always need to challenge the processes and ideas that don't make sense.

Start with a cage containing five monkeys. In the cage, hang a banana on a string and put a set of stairs under it. Before long, a monkey will go to the stairs and start to climb toward the banana. As soon as the monkey touches the stairs, spray all of the monkeys with cold water. After a while, another monkey makes an attempt with the same result—all the monkeys are sprayed with cold water.

Remove one of the monkeys from the cage and replace it with a new one. The new monkey starts up the stairs to get the banana. All the monkeys start screaming and yelling and attack the new monkey. The new monkey does not understand why the other monkeys are attacking him. The monkeys are attacking him because they do not want to be blasted with cold water again. Now replace another of the original monkeys. The new monkey sees the banana and starts to climb the stairs. To his horror, all the other monkeys, including the other new monkey, attack him. After another attempt and attack, he knows if he tries to climb the stairs, he will be assaulted. Pretty soon, when any monkey tries to climb the stairs, the other monkeys will try to prevent it.

Next, remove another of the original five monkeys and

replace it with a new one. The newcomer goes to the stairs and is attacked. The previous newcomer takes part in the punishment with enthusiasm.

Again, replace a fourth original monkey with a new one. The new one makes it to the stairs and is attacked as well while cold water is sprayed on all the monkeys. Four of the five monkeys that beat him have no idea why they were not permitted to climb the stairs or why they are participating in the beating of the newest monkey, but they do it anyway.

After replacing the fifth original monkey, all the monkeys that have been sprayed with cold water have been replaced. Nevertheless, no monkey ever again approaches the stairs. Why not? Because that's the way it's always been around here.

This is what happens. Things are done a specific way, and over time, it's forgotten why things are done that way. You end up with people just doing what they're told.

How do you rectify this?

- good comprehensive documentation
- comprehensive training at all levels
- valuing experience
- balancing outside hiring with internal promotions

Treat human resources like a financial portfolio. Balance your high-risk (external hires/contractors) investments with low-risk (internal promotion) investments.

Please don't get the impression that I'm against the use of contractors or hiring from outside the company. Contractors provide a valuable service and can fill an important need. Hiring contractors is a way to test-drive a potential hire. Contractors and outside hires bring experience from outside that can significantly aid the company, and contractors provide temporary services in times of resource constraints or productivity imbalance.

The thing is, training is knowledge, and knowledge breeds confidence and decisiveness. Experience is knowledge gained through mistakes and participation. If you have experienced and knowledgeable people working for you, you typically get better and faster decision-making. Projects progress quicker, and errors are few.

Say you have two people working for you. One has ten years of experience and a solid record. The other has been with the company for less than two years and has performed well. Which one do you think would tend to complete a task faster? Sure, this is a generalization and there are a lot of factors that go into this analogy that I have skipped over, such as attitude, drive, and so on, but let's consider these attributes are identical between the two. The point is, people with experience will tend to perform better. Their knowledge of processes, their well-developed network, and their understanding of company procedures would give them an edge.

The advantage a company has in maintaining a core competency in their product and processes is the ability to train new people and pass on experience, which helps distribute the knowledge. You don't want to have a company that operates like the monkey analogy. You want a company where experience is valued and training is as important as net profit.

Experienced people tend to carry a greater workload and process assignments at a faster rate. Would you trust someone new to an important assignment, or someone you know has experience and with whom you've previously worked? Training also helps in providing more available resources for assignments, a greater pool of resources to draw from rather than always returning to the same person or persons.

There's a balance between the past and the future. We learn from the past to innovate for the future.

45

Management

AT A COMPANY I worked at, as part of the austerity program management instituted, we weren't allowed to travel unless we had a very good reason. We needed to fill out a form, get it approved, and then book our tickets. Tickets needed to be booked a month in advance to get the best pricing. I guess management thought engineers trying to fix production problems were just traveling for fun and not really doing anything that couldn't be done through conference calls.

The irony was that management traveled practically every week. Why? If anyone could accomplish a job over the phone, it's management. Discussing high-level strategies doesn't require you to be on-site. See the hypocrisy in their policy? We engineers were so handcuffed in accomplishing our tasks that more errors and delays occurred. Meanwhile, management was traveling and complaining about travel budgets.

If management insisted that they needed to meet face-to-face to adequately engage in meaningful discussions, why

would this not be applicable to those trying to resolve manufacturing problems or complete time-sensitive projects? The
logic does not work, especially if you are a global company.
Travel is a necessary part of doing business for a global company. You need to establish personal rapport between individuals at the sites. Trust and working relationships can only
be developed face-to-face. This expedites cooperation that
allows deadlines to be realized and work to be conducted and
completed as anticipated.

Here are a few examples to help illustrate my point.

We were experiencing product complaints due to varia-
tions. An investigation was initiated to find the root cause.
The team reviewed specifications and procedures but could
not find anything wrong or missing. The manufacturing site
was asked if the testing was being done correctly. Did they
observe the process? Were the operators doing the steps according to procedures? The manufacturing site replied that
everything was being done properly.

It was puzzling. What could be wrong? The team decided
they needed to visit the manufacturing site to see for themselves. This proved to be a smart call. The team arrived and
went out to the manufacturing floor to observe the operators.
The operators were performing the task correctly, but the
team noticed that the machine was not closing correctly. They
checked the tooling and found the dies were worn. The dies
were not being maintained correctly. New dies were installed,
and the problem immediately disappeared.

This is an example of where the team could not resolve
the problem remotely. It was only possible by direct observa-
tion. In this case there was a die inspection procedure, but it
was not being followed properly. This was asked about at the
onset of the investigation, to which the manufacturing site

replied the procedure was indeed being followed and they had their records. Trust, but verify.

In another example, we were trying to understand why a manufacturing site halfway around the world was not getting the same results as we were for a particular test. Conference calls were held, and questions and responses went back and forth with no solution presenting itself. This went on for some time with no progress. We eventually got permission to travel to the site. We found that the site was not using the right setup. They thought they were. Part of the problem in communication was language barriers. It was only when we were able to observe in person did we find out the cause of the problem. Yes, we tried videoing the test, but the problem was very subtle and not showing up in the video. Our presence also helped develop trust and open up channels of communications that were a benefit moving forward. The site did not mind asking for help, knowing we were there to support them.

Management needs to realize that there are some things that must be accepted as part of doing business to be effective and viable in day-to-day operations. This also helps ensure consistency and harmonization among similar manufacturing systems by the transfer of best practices—something that individuals are more apt to do if they have a personal relationship in place.

Closing Remarks

I hope you've come away with some ideas that will help you in your career and with office politics. I realize that everyone weighs factors differently, but this is a summation of what I have experienced and what I have seen work and fail.

Your experiences will be different from mine. Your learning may come easily or may be the result of difficult lessons. Regardless, learning is a sign of growth. I hope you have the chance to pass on what you learn to help someone else jump-start his or her career.

As cultures change and society adapts to an ever-changing world, protocols will change and disappear.

I hope through all the ups and downs, there remains a commonality in how we interact as human beings, as coworkers, and as members of society. If that holds true, then some of what I have expressed in this book will still be relevant.

Maybe you will become one of our future leaders. If you do, please remember, as the saying goes, those who ignore the past are doomed to repeat it. If we ignore our mistakes, our experience, and our history, we will repeat our past failures in our innovation efforts. Striking the balance between the two is important. Good leaders also listen to their gut feelings.

I hope at some point in your career, you get the opportunity to pause and reflect on this book and realize, in some small way, that it helped you along your journey.

Now go forth into that maelstrom we call work. Be brave, be confident, and trust in yourself.

About the Author

Eric lives in beautiful rural Bucks County, Pennsylvania, with his wife, Kim, and their cat, Baxter. They have two grown daughters, Kara and Kasey, who are experiencing the ups and downs of working for a living. When not writing, Eric works full-time as a quality engineer for a major corporation, where he also mentors the next generation of visionaries. Eric and his wife enjoy dining out and traveling when the opportunity arises. When not traveling or working, Eric can be found out in their woods exploring nature or cycling around the neighborhood. *Perceptions and Expectations* is his debut book. He hopes to write more when he retires. Eric's wife hopes he does too so he stays out of trouble.

Connect with the Author

If you would like to email the author or inquire about bulk purchasing for classrooms or gifts, you can contact the author at ehinri76@gmail.com

Leave a Review

If you enjoyed this book, please consider writing a review on Amazon or other website. Reviews help self-published authors make their books more visible to new readers.

Acknowledgments

ANY WRITER WILL tell you a book is not solely the creation of the author, but a compilation of efforts by a multitude of people molding the manuscript into a finished book. For me, being a first-time author, it took more than just a few people. I first want to thank my mother-in-law for providing the impetus for me to start putting pen to paper or keyboard to screen, so to speak. Thanks to Deborah DeNicola for getting my manuscript off to a good start and Shayla Raquel for her invaluable insights and corrections in taking the manuscript to the next level. Thanks to William for talking me off the ledge and the whole team at Archway Publishing. Thanks to Marcia, Mary, Joe, and Kathleen for their draft reads (you know who you are!) Your feedback gave me hope and improved the content and message immensely!

Suggested Reading

Covey, Steven. *The 7 Habits of Highly Effective People*. New York: Fireside, 1989.
Great book on communications

Goldratt, Eliyahu, and Jeff Cox. *The Goal*. New York: North River Press, 1984.
Helpful book on manufacturing problem-solving

Keirsey, David, and Marilyn Bates. *Please Understand Me: Character Types and Temperament Types*. California: Prometheus Nemesis Books, 1978.
Useful workbook to identify the type of person you are based on your answers to a questionnaire

Burke, James. *Connections*. Boston: Little, Brown and Company, 1978.
Teaches how inventions and discoveries are interconnected and influential on outcomes

Rath, Tom. *Strength Finders 2.0*. New York: Gallup Press, 2007.
Shows how to find your areas of strengths